TEST PILOTS
OF THE
JET AGE

TEST PILOTS
OF THE
JET AGE

Men Who Heralded a New Era in Aviation

COLIN HIGGS and BRUCE VIGAR

AIR WORLD

AIR WORLD

TEST PILOTS OF THE JET AGE
Men Who Heralded a New Era in Aviation

First published in Great Britain in 2021 by
Air World
An imprint of
Pen & Sword Books Ltd
Yorkshire – Philadelphia

ISBN 978 1 52674 775 4

Typeset by SJmagic DESIGN SERVICES, India.

Printed and bound in the UK by CPI (UK) Ltd, Croydon, CR0 4YY.

Pen & Sword Books Limited incorporates the imprints of Atlas, Archaeology, Aviation, Discovery, Family History, Fiction, History, Maritime, Military, Military Classics, Politics, Select, Transport, True Crime, Air World, Frontline Publishing, Leo Cooper, Remember When, Seaforth Publishing, The Praetorian Press, Wharncliffe Local History, Wharncliffe Transport, Wharncliffe True Crime and White Owl.

For a complete list of Pen & Sword titles please contact

PEN & SWORD BOOKS LIMITED
47 Church Street, Barnsley, South Yorkshire, S70 2AS, England
E-mail: enquiries@pen-and-sword.co.uk
Website: www.pen-and-sword.co.uk

Or

PEN AND SWORD BOOKS
1950 Lawrence Rd, Havertown, PA 19083, USA
E-mail: Uspen-and-sword@casematepublishers.com
Website: www.penandswordbooks.com

Contents

Introduction

The day 15 July 1953 dawned cloudy but dry. Sunshine was forecast for later that morning. For the thousands of Royal Air Force personnel gathered at RAF Odiham in Hampshire, this was indeed, welcome news. For weeks they had toiled ceaselessly to prepare the airfield, living in a tented city. Now, the newly crowned Queen Elizabeth II was going to visit Odiham and 'review' the Royal Air Force.

The morning went well. As well as the men and women lined up for parade, there were 300 aircraft waiting for inspection. After lunch, the Coronation Review, as it was called, reached its climax. A staggering 600 aircraft from the RAF and other Commonwealth air forces took to the skies in a carefully choreographed series of fly-pasts. More than fifty aircraft types took part, representing every branch of the RAF. Pre-war piston engine aircraft such as the Avro Anson led the fly-past. Following them came scores of jet fighters like the de Havilland Vampire and Venom, and Gloster Meteors. They were followed by the latest Supermarine Swifts from Boscombe Down. The RAF's new jet bomber, the English Electric Canberra, was there as well as prototypes of the new V-Force, the Handley Page Victor, Vickers Valiant and the iconic Avro Vulcan. These were the aircraft that brought the RAF into the 'Jet Age' and the Coronation Review of 1953 showed the RAF at a pivotal point in its history as it made its transition into a modern jet air force.

That this change was possible was down to a small, select group of largely forgotten men who risked everything to go further, faster and higher than ever before. They were the test pilots.

Test pilots such as de Havillands' John Cunningham and English Electric's Roland Beamont were already household names due to their wartime exploits. Others including Peter Twiss, Duncan Simpson and many others became familiar names because of what they achieved in the air pushing their aircraft ever further, faster and higher. As a result, flight still captured the public imagination and crowds would flock in their tens of thousands to air shows like Farnborough to watch the pilots perform rolls, loops and soaring climbs in the latest types that were often fresh off the drawing board.

But test flying was not without its risks. Ten years before the Coronation Review, Britain became the first country in the world to establish a school specifically to train test pilots within the Aeroplane & Armament Experimental Establishment at Boscombe Down in Wiltshire. Today, it is called the Empire Test Pilots' School (ETPS) but its creation in 1943 as the Test Pilots' Training Flight was in recognition of the fact that too many pilots were being killed testing new aircraft during the Second World War. In 1945 it moved to RAF Cranfield before a move to the Royal Aircraft Establishment at Farnborough in 1947. In 1968 it moved back to Boscombe Down, where it has remained to the present day. Its mission was to 'provide suitably trained pilots for testing duties in aeronautical research and development establishments within the service and the industry'. It's a measure of just how dangerous test flying was that five pilots who graduated from the first course were killed in testing accidents.

Not all the test pilots featured in this book graduated from the Empire Test Pilots' School. Pilots such as Eric Brown and John Cunningham had already begun their test flying before the Second World War. They, like their post-war colleagues, helped establish Britain's aircraft industry stay at the forefront of aviation development as it transitioned from the piston engine era into the jet age.

And what of the aircraft? As eyes gazed skywards on that July afternoon in 1953, it was easy to see how far aircraft design had advanced. Leading the way were Gloster Meteors. The RAF had been the first Allied air force to operate jets in 1944 when they were rushed into service with No. 616 Squadron based at Manston, Kent. Prime Minister Winston Churchill was under pressure to sooth rising public alarm over the V1 flying bomb campaign that had begun in June 1944. These small cruise missiles were causing a lot of destruction as they travelled at speeds that made them difficult to shoot down both by anti-aircraft guns and fighter aircraft that simply could not accelerate quickly enough to catch them. The problem was that the piston-engine fighter had more or less reached the end of its life. Pistons could only produce a finite amount of power and the large frontal area of bigger engines coupled with straight wings meant that the aircraft were too aerodynamically inefficient to go through the air any faster. The jet engine, however, had the potential for unlimited amounts of power and as the knowledge of aerodynamics improved, aircraft were soon not only flying close to the speed of sound, they were flying past it.

The Germans had been the first to introduce jet aircraft into service in mid-1944 with the Messerschmitt Me 262. Not only was it jet powered but it also had swept wings. Although the Gloster Meteor also entered service in July 1944, it was according to those who flew the early marks no faster than the piston-engine fighters of the day. More power soon followed and the Meteor became the cornerstone of many air forces around the world as they too entered their own jet eras.

The end of the war in Europe in 1945 brought a wealth of knowledge of aerodynamics as German scientists and engineers found new positions in the west. Thus, those present on 15 July 1953 cannot have failed to notice the changing shape of aircraft from the straight-winged Meteor to a prototype of the swept-wing Hunter or even the delta wing of the mighty Vulcan prototype.

The test pilots featured in this book were all part of this 'Golden Age' of British aviation. Their comments and observations are theirs and theirs alone. They do not necessarily follow the prescribed path of an official history, but it is clear that they all felt that they were part of something that was pioneering, that they were rolling back the frontiers of flight in leaps and bounds. Their observations are drawn from a deep well of experience. Although they are all British, many served as exchange pilots in other countries, particularly the United States. Most saw combat in the Second World War and all of them ended their careers with hundreds of types recorded in their log books. Most had learned their trade in ancient biplanes but finished their careers in aircraft that could go faster than the speed of sound.

After the war, the reputation of Britain's aircraft industry for innovation, research and quality shone bright. The aircraft they produced pushed back the frontiers of flight, set new records and were sold to other countries, helping them into their own jet era. But such success was all too brief. The Defence White Paper prepared by Duncan Sandys in 1957 proposed replacing fighters with missiles. Almost overnight orders were cancelled, research cut right back. It all but killed off Britain's independent aircraft manufacturers. Some sought sanctuary in mergers and takeovers, one or two others tried to go it alone. Gradually the great names of Gloster, Fairey, Handley Page, Hawker, Supermarine and others were consigned to history.

Jim Cooksey

Jim Cooksey joined the Royal Air Force in 1926 as a fifteen-year-old apprentice before training as a pilot in 1936. His wartime career ended in Australia before returning to Britain to take command of No. 74 Squadron at the beginning of 1946. Cooksey was to oversee its transition into a front-line Meteor squadron. But first, he had to familiarise himself with this new type of propulsion:

> The circumstances were that we wanted to see what it was like so they brought one [the single-engined E.28/39] down for us to try out. It was very interesting because when it first flew it was on a grass airfield and the stack pipe on it was only a small diameter, very low-powered Whittle engine and the chap opened it full out and it just didn't move. He beckoned the ground crew over as he couldn't get started so they gave him a push and he got going. It was an experience but one realised how low powered the first jets were.

Cooksey's RAF career was nearing its end and in 1947 he applied to Glosters for a job as a test pilot:

> I needed to earn my bread and butter and what else would I do? I only knew how to fly and I flew down on my last day with the squadron to Glosters to see Bill Waterton, chief test pilot, and he said as they were not getting enough Meteors out he'd already got another pilot. I read in the paper the next day he got killed half an hour after I left so I rang him (Bill Waterton) up and that's how I joined Glosters.

Back then speed records brought great prestige to the country as well as the manufacturers. For the pilots it brought adulation as the newsreels brought news of their exploits to an astounded public. Cooksey had been testing Gloster's new Meteor Mk 8 and hoped to capture foreign sales in the face of stiffening competition from the United States. The 1,000km closed-circuit speed record had been held for four years by a United States Air Force P-80 Shooting Star jet fighter. Glosters felt that the Meteor Mk 8 might be the aircraft to wrest the title back.

Cooksey made a number of practice flights and it became clear that fuel was going to be marginal. After weeks of poor weather, on 12 May 1950 conditions seemed perfect. At 5pm he flashed over the airfield's starting line at 150ft. The attempt was now on:

> I used to do a lot of flying in those days and every time I flew I used to practise various aspects of it and reckoned that if I was at 35,000ft at Tewkesbury I could do a dead-stick landing if I dragged the fuel out a little bit too much. I remember practising quite a lot and waiting quite a long time to get the weather perfect. I wanted fine weather all the way up to Fife Ness, Fife Ness being on the North Shore of Loch Ness in the Firth of Forth. I waited for perfect conditions, then took off I think about six o'clock one night, thought this is it, have a bash. I came back down by the official observers down there (so that the observers representing the International Aeronautical Federation could identify his aircraft). I then climbed up again and stayed up there at 35,000ft. I juggled the fuel consumption. If I thought it was getting a bit low I went up 5,000ft. Less speed but less consumption. I then called up and said I was over Wenlock Edge, which was a well-known mark, and I remember saying that I'll be at Moreton Valence in approximately seventeen minutes, which I hit almost to the dot. I landed back at Moreton Valence with 17 gallons to spare so I cut it fairly fine. 17 out of 700!

Cooksey had covered the distance in one hour, twelve minutes and 58.2 seconds, with a recorded speed of 510.9mph. At first Cooksey was disappointed as he felt he could have gone faster but it was a new world record and one that would stand for another six years. What made his achievement all the more impressive was that the Mk 8 that he flew was an aircraft straight off the production line.

JIM COOKSEY

Jim Cooksey's career as a test pilot finished when Meteor production ended in 1957. In that time he formed a clear idea about what made a good test pilot. They are qualities that we were to hear many times while recording the interviews that appear in this book:

> Well, you had to be a good pilot for one thing, and I think you had to have a methodical brain and be noting performance ratings down accurately and things like that. I don't think it was a matter of being more devoted to the actual purpose of testing and not just having a jolly flying aeroplane around.

John Cunningham

John Cunningham was one of those pilots whose testing career began before the Second World War. Born on 27 July 1917 in Croydon on the outskirts of London, his passion for flying began as a child when, at the age of nine, he was taken up for a ride in an Avro 504 biplane. His enthusiasm was further stimulated at Whitgift School, which was near Croydon airport:

> I was determined to be involved with aeroplanes. I didn't know in what capacity and it wasn't until I was about sixteen or so that I said I thought I really would like to go to Cranwell to join the RAF. It was only then that my mother (my father died when I was a twelve-year-old) said that my father didn't want me to have a service career. I didn't know that until then and I know I thought that was disappointing. But, anyway, I was determined to do something with aeroplanes and so I thought I would try and arrange to join some company and have training. I approached one or two, one of which was the de Havilland technical school, in early 1935. I went for an interview and they accepted me to join the technical school in the summer of 1935.
>
> By good fortune, soon after I had been accepted for this technical training with de Havillands, a friend of the family who had been a founder member of the Middlesex Auxiliary Air Force squadron, knowing that I was keen on aeroplanes, asked me if I had ever thought of joining the Auxiliary Air Force. Well, I had never thought anything about it and he said that as he was at the end of his five years and had to give up his place, would I be interested? If I was, he would arrange for me to have an interview with the C/O of the squadron because I would be taught to fly by them at Hendon and

4

I would become a member of 604 Squadron. I said that was marvellous and that I would love to take this on if he could arrange this interview, which he did. I was accepted and joined the Middlesex Squadron at Hendon in the latter part of 1935 and was taught to fly there.

No. 604 (County of Middlesex) Squadron had been formed in March 1930 and received its first Airco DH.9A aircraft the following month. The squadron had been assigned the role of day bombing and by July 1934 it was operating the Sidney Camm-designed Hawker Hart. However, the Hart's performance was such that it could outperform the fighters of the day and so a fighter variant was developed called the Demon. Following its reassignment as a two-seater fighter squadron, No. 604 Squadron's Harts were replaced with Demons during the summer of 1935. On 15 March 1936 Cunningham made his first solo flight. Then, on 7 May, he was commissioned as a pilot officer in the Royal Air Force. Cunningham's experience of learning to fly in the Auxiliary Air Force was to stand him in good stead in his career at de Havilland.

The company had established a fine reputation for innovation with aircraft like the Moth, which revolutionised general aviation during the 1920s. In the 1930s the Fox Moth was the first commercial transport to operate without government subsidy:

> Having completed my technical training, the department I joined at Hatfield was the DH.94 Moth Minor department. That was a two-seater, low-wing monoplane trainer. As I had by then three years of flying and at de Havilland there were only three test pilots in total and the Moth Minor department that I was in was just starting its production line of aircraft, Sir Geoffrey de Havilland or the 'Captain' de Havilland as he then was, knowing my flying experience, said that he would like me to take on the production test flying of this aeroplane as in my department we were putting them together and I should continue to fly them. It would help his son with the enormous load of work he'd got on production flying all de Havilland's production aeroplanes. The only danger was the one that one faced with flying anyway, so there was nothing extraordinary about it.

The 1930s saw the growth of civilian aviation. Gradually the world was opened up by air travel as more routes became established. Aircraft like the de

Havilland Dragon Rapide, which was a small, economical short-haul transport capable of carrying six to eight passengers, were central to this expansion:

> The company was growing, and it was very busy because it produced successful light aircraft and small transports and was in the midst of producing and building the large four-engine transport, the Albatross, and followed by the twin-engine Flamingo, which was the first all-metal aeroplane de Havillands had built.
>
> Sir Geoffrey was a very practical, farsighted man who liked his flying and regularly flew himself away at weekends to his weekend home, and he would come back on Monday in his Leopard Moth, usually, back to Hatfield.
>
> He wasn't very popular with (the Air Ministry) because he always rather opposed their views on many ideas about what their new aircraft should be.
>
> Captain de Havilland realised that if an aeroplane was going to be fast and do its job successfully it had to be streamlined, fairly lightish in weight and not carry a lot of heavy armament with it if it was going to have a high performance. So, he did not feel at all happy with the requirements for heavy armament on the bombers with gun turrets and large crews, and he cited as his example the original Comet that won the London to Australia race in 1934 as being a streamlined, twin-engined, two-seater aeroplane that had a fine performance and really it was that that convinced him that any military aircraft ought to follow those lines.
>
> He persuaded the Air Ministry to allow him to go ahead and build what turned out to be the Mosquito, which was perhaps the fastest and most successful wartime design and developed aeroplane that we had in the 39– 45 war.
>
> It was a very successful aeroplane built in very large numbers with a very low loss rate because it had fighter-like speed.

During the summer of 1939 it became clear that war with Germany was all but inevitable. Cunningham was testing Dragons when the RAF mobilised at the end of August 1939. He faced a difficult decision: should he give up his testing career at de Havilland or re-join his squadron? In the end he decided the latter as, he reasoned, it was the RAF who had taught him to fly and he would be more useful to them than test flying. Cunningham re-joined No. 604 Squadron as it prepared for war. The squadron was now equipped with the Bristol Blenheim.

But Cunningham's role as a test pilot was far from on hold. During the summer of 1940 he was tasked with testing a mine armed with a photo-electric fuse. The plan was to drop these on top of bomber formations. However, this project was abandoned, In July 1940 the squadron was redesignated as a specialist night fighter unit and Cunningham was promoted to acting squadron leader, commanding 'B' Flight:

> The Blenheim was a nice flying aeroplane, but it wasn't designed in any way as a night fighter. It had a series of glass-fronted panels in the nose and it was not at all good for looking out of. I remember one of my rather competent pilots saying that all he could see when he looked out of his Blenheim at night was his white, frightened face looking back at him because there was so many panels of glass that reflected the face and that was a fairly good description of what the Blenheim night fighter was like and we didn't have radar when we got our Blenheims.
>
> We had nothing to help us at night except perhaps, searchlights and they were not at all satisfactory because our weather here in winter is mainly cloudy and until radar came along we had virtually no defence against night. Anti-aircraft fire made a big flash and a bang but wasn't very effective and so we started off with no real defence at night until after the day battles finished in September 1940.

With little more than eyesight, training and instinct to guide them, hunting down night-time German raiders seemed a hopeless task:

One idea that was tried out was the Turbinlite. A radar-equipped Douglas Havoc was fitted with a large searchlight in the nose. In conjunction with ground radar, the Havoc would locate the enemy and attempt to formate with a Hurricane. As they got closer, the Havoc was to illuminate the enemy aircraft so that the Hurricane could then shoot it down. As the Havoc had to have all its defensive armament removed in order to carry the radar, it made a very good target for German gunners once the light came on:

> The Turbinlite was ridiculous because we already had the capability without any lights but using radar following and closing in on an aeroplane and the last thing in the world one

wanted to do was advertise your presence by shining a great big light. It was useless trying to formate at night.

The night fighter had to have his own armament so that it could shoot at whatever the target was. To have a couple of fighters formating that might or might not still be there after you had gone up through cloud was just so stupid it's hardly true!

Eventually, when I got 85 Squadron I was told we were going to receive a Mosquito with a Turbinlite so I went straight to see the C-in-C, Fighter Command (Sir Roderick Hill) and said, 'Look, this is the most appalling waste of time and money and everything else. Apart from being totally unsuitable.' I had flown the aeroplane at night just so that I could say that I had flown in it and I told him that I was not going to operate it. The C-in-C said that he accepted my feelings on it and said that we would ground that Turbinlite and that was the end of it. That was 1943. It is unbelievable that it got as far as the Mosquito.

However, there was light at the end of the tunnel as No. 604 Squadron was among the first to receive a new experimental Airborne Interception Radar system (AI). The system needed a second crew to operate and although Blenheims could accommodate the system, the aeroplane was just too slow to intercept German raiders.

In October 1940 things began to improve when the squadron received its first Bristol Beaufighters. The Beaufighter was powerful enough to catch bombers and by working through some exercises with Ground Control of Interception (GCI), Cunningham and his operator Jimmy Rawnsley began to see some success. At 10,000ft, the Beaufighter's AI system had an effective range of about 4 miles and a minimum altitude of 400ft. Working with GCI, which could get them to within a mile of their target, Cunningham and Rawnsley would then use the AI system to bring them directly astern and slightly below the enemy aircraft. By staying below the target, the Beaufighter stayed out of the slipstream and was masked by the dark ground below it. Once they had got close enough, Cunningham would open fire. That first burst was usually enough to end the engagement:

We got radar into our aeroplanes and the first night fighter that was effective was the Bristol Beaufighter. That had good cannons, four 20mm cannon and radar and we achieved a great deal in 1941 and '42.

It was then apparent that the German aircraft were getting faster and the Mosquito came in, which was nearly 100mph faster than the Beaufighter, and that continued throughout until the end of the war, and we were then very well organised in night-fighting.

The shape of the Mosquito was down to the chief designer, who had to come up with the most streamlined shape that he could that would still allow the crew to operate and see out and do their job, and it was all determined by the need for the aircraft to have a high performance and not have undue drag, which usually went with unsightly as well. So, a streamlined shape – and the Mosquito was a lovely shape – and that was determined by it having to have a high speed.

The Mosquito's cockpit only just had enough room for two. Getting into one today one realises how confined one's space was compared to what is accepted today.

By the end of the war Cunningham had shot down twenty aircraft with a further three probable and six damaged. He had also attained the rank of group captain in command of night operations at 11 Group RAF. At twenty-six years old he was one of the youngest to hold that rank. Although he was offered a permanent commission following the end of the war, he decided that a career as a senior officer in the peacetime RAF was not for him.

As well as proving a formidable combat pilot, he had also demonstrated his abilities to test aircraft and analyse their capabilities:

De Havillands asked me and tried to get me released or at least get a demobilisation date because they said they would like me to come and take a part in our operation at Hatfield. I was very happy to return to Hatfield and so I declined the offer of a permanent commission in the Air Force so that I could go back, when demobilisation came, to Hatfield and I was happy to do that.

I was still in the Air Force in 1944 when I was asked to go and fly (the Vampire) at Farnborough and that was the first jet that I flew and there was no shadow of doubt that it was a marvellous way to be driven through the sky by jet. Nice and smooth and fast. No shadow of doubt that jets were definitely going to take over (from piston power) totally, which of course, they did because of the advance in every way and the simplicity of them was marked.

The twin boom [on the Vampire] made it straightforward for the jet exhaust to go out unobstructed at the tail end and the twin booms carried the tail and rudder that were so necessary.

You could see straight out the front through a bulletproof screen because there was no big engine in front of you and it was a very straightforward flying machine; nice controls, very responsive and it had a nose wheel, so that it was on three wheels on the ground, as opposed to a tailwheel, and it was an absolute joy to fly and so clearly a version of that as a night fighter would be an ideal way of developing the night fighter.

A night fighter was usually a twin-engine aeroplane with a radome or aerials in the nose (or later a radome) and it needed two people. There was the radar operator and pilot preferably sitting side by side as in the Mosquito, and so if the Vampire development as a night fighter turned out to have a nose like the Mosquito plus the four cannon, 20mm cannon that the Mosquito had, it would be an ideal aeroplane as a night fighter.

It perhaps could have done with more fuel because, inevitably, being a small aeroplane it couldn't carry as much fuel as the Mosquito carried, which was a big twin-engine propeller aeroplane, of course.

The radar system was immensely developed. It went through from its very first stages in 1940, which were rather unreliable equipment and limited range and capability. It was immensely developed and became a very fine piece of equipment at the end of the war with [10cm] equipment, which was reliable, had longer range and gave a wonderful return.

I think we had night-fighter Vampires on production at Hatfield. I think it was 1946/47.

Generally, the Vampire was looked on as being at the early development stage of the jet fighter and one that was fairly simple and could be operated by some of the smaller countries that didn't have such huge demands on high-performance aeroplanes.

To a large extent that's what people wanted them for because there wasn't much demand for heavy bombers, attack, and so on from countries that didn't have huge requirements for military activities.

10

The Vampire was followed into service by the Venom. It was designed as a single-seat fighter-bomber as well as a two-seat night fighter, which was created by taking a Venom night-fighter fuselage and adding the Venom's wings, engine and boom and tail section:

> The Venom was a bigger version of the Vampire, really. It was still basically on the same lines as the Vampire. It had a thinner wing and went faster than the Vampire.
>
> The Venom had a bigger de Havilland engine, the Ghost engine, and it was that engine that we also used in the Comet, which was Hatfield's first four-engine commercial jet airliner.
>
> Of course, we then had ideas on further development and the later aeroplane became the DH.110, which was a much more powerful twin-engined jet that first flew in 1951.

In many ways, the Venom with its thin wings and slightly swept leading edge was a transitional design as the RAF moved from the first-generation jets like the Gloster Meteor and the de Havilland Vampire. A greater understanding of aerodynamics and access to data from captured German scientists meant that a new generation of aircraft led by the Hawker Hunter was now on the drawing board:

> German data had all gone in as soon as the end of the war came. We learnt all that we could from German developments and I think the world demand for higher-performance aircraft meant that we looked to take the greatest advantage that we could. So, there was always the demand for improved performance and range and Hatfield felt that it had a chance of benefiting from that.
>
> The post-war years was a time of constant development and improvement and one of the improvements, the very first plane that I flew, was on the replacement DH.108, which was the tailless research aircraft that we built at Hatfield in 1947. So, up to that time there had been no ejection seats in any Hatfield aeroplane but from then on, of course, it became standard in the military aeroplanes.
>
> The DH.108 project was to learn all that we could from swept wings and from German developments that had gone on during the war. This tailless research aircraft had the

jet engine that was in the Vampire and swept wings. We learnt from the 108 the immensely high performance that wing could give. But the stability of the aeroplane was not adequate for development into either a commercial airliner or military aircraft as we at that time were not able to produce artificial stability, which, of course, later in the development of aircraft became something that is relatively normal practice. So, although the 108 had fine performance, it didn't have the necessary stability under turbulent conditions that we needed, and it was a demanding aeroplane in that its handling at low speed, particularly at the stalling end of the flying business, was not really terribly satisfactory.

We learnt our lesson sharply that there was a need for a conventional tail and that the high sweep – the link between low and high sweep of the wing – on the 108 was not the ideal solution for what was to become the Comet and it was very clear that the 108 layout was not to be suitable for development of the Comet. So, that was the biggest lesson we learnt from that.

There wasn't very much that we took from the 108 to develop the Vampire and Venom because it was the aircraft that followed that from which we learnt and developed and that in the military role became the DH.110, eventually becoming the Sea Vixen fighter.

The RAF had a requirement which the 110 and the Gloster Javelin filled, but partly because the DH factories were so full and busy with varying aeroplanes and developments, Glosters were able to produce the Javelin because they did not have many competing aeroplanes.

The Javelin had its handling problems, but I think the Sea Vixen had the performance with the large tail on two booms.

John Derry's crash at Farnborough was a tragedy that set us back inevitably, but the aeroplane itself continued as the Sea Vixen and did its job reasonably well.

In fact, the Sea Vixen was to remain in service until 1972, when it was replaced by the McDonnell Douglas Phantom FG.1.

On 27 September 1946, chief test pilot Geoffrey de Havilland, the founder's son, was killed when the DH.108 Swallow he was flying broke up over the Thames Estuary. Cunningham was subsequently promoted to the post of chief test pilot just as the first DH.106 Comet prototype was nearing completion. The Comet was the world's first jet airliner and on 27 July 1949 the Comet made its maiden flight with Cunningham at the controls. The world of civilian air transport had now entered the jet age:

> The Comet project began because there was a committee set up at the end of the war to establish what types of aeroplanes the British aircraft industry should produce. The Comet was one of them – a transatlantic mail or passenger-carrying jet – and it was with that in view that the Comet went forward.
>
> I think de Havilland got the Comet contract because of the aircraft it had built before the war and during the war, particularly the Mosquito.
>
> The Comet's development phase went extremely well because of all the new features that we used in the Comet, and one of them was powered controls and, of course, the Ghost engine, which was a larger version of the Goblin that was in the Vampire. All these items were in flying aircraft in the two, three, four years before the Comet first flew, so that we had thoroughly proved to ourselves the success of the new features that were going to be put into the one aeroplane, the Comet. So, when it first flew it was a great joy to know that the new items had all been developed and thoroughly tested by us at Hatfield.
>
> The Mk 1 Comet was the last to carry a de Havilland engine because of development, particularly by Rolls-Royce, which was more advanced than anyone else in producing a jet engine that had the increased power and efficiency, fuel efficiency in particular. So it was quite clear that the development of the Comet 1 (which had de Havilland jet engines) when fitted with the Rolls-Royce engine would have longer range and slightly higher performance. That was a line to follow
>
> The great advantage from a piloting point of view was that you had a much greater range on the fuel that the Comet carried. It also had more power and you had very good take-off and climb performance, particularly in hot climates. So that there's no shadow of doubt that the improved engine performance that you got from the Rolls engine really made the Comet into a must-have for the airlines.

The Comet was designed particularly for take-off in hot and high climates and my immediate comparison was that although the (Boeing) 707 prototype was a fine flying aeroplane, it didn't have the very smart take-off and climb that we had on the Comet because we had rather more power for the weight that we were carrying than the original 707.

The Canadians had two or three, I can't remember, but they certainly had two Comet 1s and they gave very good service over a long time flying from Canada down to Germany for the Canadian Air Force.

The Comet set a new standard for air travel. Before the Comet, air travel was not a particularly comfortable experience. Aircraft were often converted wartime bombers or adapted freighters driven by noisy piston engines. The Comet was about 50 per cent faster than the most advanced piston-engined aircraft and its better rate of climb reduced flight times even further. In its first year of service Comets carried around 30,000 passengers. The de Havilland Ghost jet engines enabled the Comet to fly high above the weather its piston-engined rivals had to fly through. At 30,000ft, the Comet was also more fuel efficient. What's more, with lower operating costs, Comets could be profitable with a load capacity of 43 per cent. As well as bringing together new technologies such as jet power, hydraulic flying controls and a pressurised cabin, there was the look: the sleek fuselage and swept-back wings and the four jet engines buried in the wing roots made the Comet look like something out of the future. Instead of little portholes, passengers could gaze down on the world below from large square windows:

> I think, quite possibly that we at de Havillands were so busy and really overwhelmed with demands for production of Comet airliners and we weren't able to produce enough quickly enough to satisfy everyone that wanted them.

The future for air travel and in particular, Britain's aviation industry looked bright. Orders were coming in from airlines all over the world. An extended and more powerful version – the Comet 2 – was already on the drawing board and a Comet 3 was on the horizon that would enable jet-powered transatlantic services to begin. Then came the accidents. At first it seemed that pilots were not used to hydraulic controls. They complained of a lack of 'feel'. Then came the inexplicable and catastrophic mid-air explosions.

All Comets were withdrawn from service and orders for the new longer-range Comet 2 cancelled. Eventually, the cause of the accidents was identified as structural failure as a result of weakness around the square windows. De Havilland embarked on an intensive programme to design and build a new Comet that was both stronger and larger than the previous version. The square windows of the Comet 1 were replaced by oval versions and the skin of the fuselage thickened slightly. The new Comet 2 first flew in 1953:

> I don't think the RAF were less enthusiastic because when the Comet 2 came on the scene, which was fitted with Rolls-Royce engines, the RAF then had a squadron of Comet 2s.

But it was not until 1958 that commercial airlines would resume Comet flights. By now the type had been developed into the Mk 4 variant and was to be the company's most successful version.

The type first flew on 27 April 1958, gaining its Certificate of Airworthiness on 24 September that same year. The very next day, the first of nineteen Comet 4s was delivered to BOAC. On 4 October, BOAC inaugurated the world's first jet-powered transatlantic service between London and New York, even though a refuelling stop was required at Newfoundland when flying westwards. The company certainly gained a lot of good publicity and orders from other international airlines were coming in. But the glory days were short-lived. The time that the Comet had been grounded enabled Boeing to catch up. By the end of October 1958, Pan Am was operating Boeing 707s on the same route. The American jets were larger, faster, longer-ranged and more cost-effective than the Comet. But the Comet's demise was still some years away and for de Havilland and Cunningham there were plenty of orders waiting to be fulfilled:

> It was a question of being able to build up a team of test pilots because we had to have quite a number who had the background and experience to do their job, whether it was on the military side or the airliner side, and so that was very demanding because we had to supply pilots to train the new airlines that had not had a jet and that was quite a big problem.
>
> The pilots would have to go for some time with the new airline whatever part of the world they were in to train their pilots and to satisfy their licensing authorities in those countries

that they were then safe to operate a jet, and so one had to have quite a number of pilots of good skills and competence to go and take part in that job.

They had to be able to get on well with people of all nationalities. They had to have confidence and skill and be people who could accept that it would take quite a time for these different countries' airlines in their different parts of the world to be happy that when they launched off that company or the airline that they were safe and that they would give a good, safe service with our aeroplane.

We didn't lose out entirely (to Boeing). We learnt a great deal from the failure of the Comet and then its later development and yes, it was a big blow and it was disappointing, but it wasn't total disaster for the industry.

Boeing were able to develop the 707 into a very good transport with improvements in engine power and in every way. They are a first-class company; they benefited from our problems and produced something that still is today, a very good transport.

Although Cunningham and his team of test pilots at Hatfield were busy helping airlines around the world transition into the jet age with the Comet, a new passenger jet was already in development.

The DH.121, or Trident as it became known, was the world's first three-engine jet. After many delays due to changes of specification, the Trident flew for the first time on 9 January 1962:

> The Trident – the last passenger jet that I was involved in – was ordered by BEA, whose main requirement was to operate in the European area, which was provided with good, long airfields. It didn't have the very long-distance flights or the hot and high airfields such as in Africa to deal with, so BEA wanted a high-speed aeroplane, economical, without the very long-range or high-altitude capability from an airfields' point of view.
>
> From a piloting point of view, it was a delightful flying aeroplane. It didn't have the range of the Comet or perhaps its short-distance take-off capability but it gave a very satisfactory answer to BEA's requirement, which was high speed in Europe. But that unfortunately got rather curtailed because so many

aeroplanes in Europe on limited routes had about the same speed.

There was certainly a demand for greater speed but as the airways got more crowded and aeroplanes had to fly on particular routes it was inevitable that speed alone would not be satisfactory because they had to fit in with a worldwide pattern of aeroplanes all flying somewhere around the same speed except, of course, in the case of the Concorde, which had this far greater height at which it flew so that there were very few aeroplanes flying at that height at that very high speed and that picture still applies really.

By the time the Trident entered service, Britain's aircraft industry had gone through dramatic change. Put simply, there were just too many manufacturers chasing a diminishing number of orders. Under pressure from central government, companies were persuaded to merge. Although the de Havilland company had produced some of aviation's most advanced designs, the high-profile tragic accidents with the Comet doomed its long-term prospects of remaining independent. In 1960, the company was swallowed up by Hawker Siddeley. By 1963 the famous 'DH' became 'HS', although the name 'de Havilland' lives on in the hundreds of Moths of various types that are still flying throughout the world to this day:

I don't think the British aircraft industry was (moving too fast), it was moving ahead and learning the whole time and it continued its development until many years after the war. As a country too many aeroplanes were, arguably, built by too many different companies and perhaps we would have been better off to concentrate on those that had proved successful in the past.

When I look back on this period I think how fortunate I was to have taken part in such a marvellous development of aviation or slightly longer than that, maybe sixty years, but I've been fortunate to have taken part in all that's gone on during that time. If I had to pick a particular favourite I suppose almost inevitably it would be the Comet. The advent of the commercial jet is a period that has perhaps given us the best out of developments in aviation for this last fifty years or so and I've been very fortunate to enjoy and take part in that.

John Cunningham enjoyed a long career in aviation. He remained chief test pilot for Hawker Siddeley right up to 1978 when it merged into British Aerospace. Apart from once having to bail out of a Moth Minor in 1939, he had enjoyed a charmed existence at a time when many of his peers were killed in flying accidents. But in 1975 his luck nearly ran out following a bird strike while taking off from Dunsfold in a DH.125. On board were several Chinese executives, with whom de Havilland had been doing good business with the Trident. Touching down at 130mph, the aircraft slithered along the runway, bursting through a hedge at the end. Unfortunately, a car was passing at that moment and was struck by the aircraft, killing the four people inside. None of the aircraft's passengers were hurt, although Cunningham sustained two crushed vertebrae. Within a year he was flying again. He eventually retired from British Aerospace in 1980, devoting himself to promoting aviation to young people and supporting the RAF Benevolent Fund. His achievements in aviation were widely recognised. He was appointed OBE in 1951 and CBE in 1963. He was awarded the DSO in 1941 and Bars in 1942 and 1944; the DFC and Bar in 1941, also the Air Efficiency Award (AE). He also held the Soviet Order of Patriotic War 1st Class and the US Silver Star. John Cunningham died on 23 July 2002, aged eighty-four.

Eric Brown

The early years of jet flight was a heroic time. Like the pioneers of flight's early years, it was not without considerable risk and many died as they sought to master this new form of technology. Eric 'Winkle' Brown was among the very best, the archetypal test pilot, if there could ever be such a thing. He certainly had all the right qualities. He was a flier of extraordinary skill and versatility, and flew 487 types between the 1930s and '80s, a world record. He also had a prodigious attention to detail but had the power to improvise. These qualities, plus an extraordinary depth of courage, transformed aviation at a critical moment in its history. His career began during the 1930s in aircraft that marked the end of the biplane era. His passion for flying was ignited during a trip to Germany before the outbreak of the Second World War:

> Well, I really came from an aviation background in the sense that my father had been in the Royal Flying Corps and then in the RAF and, of course, with this background you're always encouraged to think along these lines.
>
> A real turning point came when my father said to me that he had been invited to a 'do' in Germany that was going to coincide with the Olympic Games, this was in 1936. He said that Ernst Udet, who was the second top-scoring fighter pilot of World War 1 after Richthofen and a complete extrovert, had decided he was going to have a 'do' at the Olympic Games with ex-combatants from World War 1. So, he invited those he could find and we were all going to have a 'hooley' in Berlin. So, my father wrote to him and asked if he could bring me and he said he's not a youngster, he's seventeen now. So, we got the 'nod' and out we went.
>
> Of course, Udet had a little 'sideshow' going on, if you'd like to call it that, while the Olympics were going on. There was

19

a little airfield nearby and he had for example, Hanna Reitsch, who was the world gliding champion at that time, giving a very nice little aerobatic show in a glider and he, of course, gave one of his absolutely magnificent aerobatic shows in a Bücker Jungmeister

During that time, after a few days, I thought he was just ignoring me, but he didn't. He spoke to me a lot. He had a rather halting English and I had schoolboy German so between us it was a bit of a halting conversation, but we got along on that and he asked me if I would like to come flying with him and I said I would love it. He then said that he was going to take me to an airfield called Halle and that he had a little two-seater out there now that he would give me a flight in it.

So we drove down to Halle and there he had a Bücker Jungmann, which was a two-seat aircraft, and he put me in the front cockpit and he flew it from the back. We went off and he then showed me his aerobatic skills. My stomach was churning around quite a bit because of all this but I managed not to 'toss my cookies', but it was a near thing and finally he came into land. I must tell you that before we took off he seemed to be very fussy about having me strapped in properly in the front, of course, for all these aerobatics but when we came into the circuit and straightened up in order to land he turned the aircraft upside down and approached inverted. I thought we were coming down so close to the ground I thought he's had a heart attack and he's just lost control and this is going to be the end. But he gave himself just enough height to turn it round, twist it round and plonk it onto the runway. Then he just roared with laughter because he knew I was sitting petrified in the front cockpit. But, after we landed we got out and he clapped me on the back and said that I will be a good fighter pilot but he said I had to learn the fighter pilot greeting and he slapped me on the back and said 'Hals und Beinbruch' [Break a leg], that's what fighter pilots say to each other, and then he drove me back to Berlin.

On the way back he said to me there were two things he would like me to do if I wanted to be a real fighter pilot. First, I could come and see him again but I would have to learn German – proper German, not schoolboy German, and secondly, I would have to learn to fly.

20

When I went back I was going to Edinburgh university to do modern languages so I joined the university air squadron and once I got there I was really hooked because we were flying the sort of aeroplanes I'd always dreamt about, which was the Gloster Gauntlet. These were the days of the rather nice biplanes – a lot of very interesting ones around like the Gauntlet and the Gladiator and the Fury and they were really quite – what should I say? – halcyon days really.

In early 1939, Brown was back in Germany, this time as an exchange teacher. He was there on 3 September, the day war broke out, and was promptly detained and questioned. Fortunately, he kept quiet about his flying experience and he was deported back to England via Switzerland complete with his MG sports car! As he was informed by the RAF that they 'were in no rush for his services', Brown decided to join the Fleet Air Arm:

In September 1939, the aircraft carrier *Courageous* was sunk in the Irish Sea with a heavy loss of Fleet Air Arm pilots. A notice went up on the board at Drem saying that the Fleet Air Arm was very short of pilots as a result of this disaster and if anybody would like to move over, would they append their names, which I did. I thought I would be popped straight into a carrier and into action. But nothing like that happened as the Navy decided to retrain me more or less into their methods of carrier operations.

When I went into the Fleet Air Arm I was posted to a fighter squadron and we were located up at Donibristle up on the Firth of Forth. We weren't quite sure what our task was going to be but then we were soon informed that we were going aboard the first escort carrier to be built, HMS *Audacity*, which was a very small ship really. It had formerly been a German banana boat that was captured in the Caribbean and the top sliced off and the flight deck put on. There was no hangar. The flight deck total length was only 420ft, which was about half the average fleet carrier's length at that time, and only two main arrestor wires. There was a third one that we called the 'For Christ's sake' wire, which was the desperate one. If you caught that and pulled it out, the crash barrier collapsed, and you ran over it. So, in practical terms there were only two arrestor wires.

Although the Fleet Air Arm began the war equipped with obsolete aircraft, Brown's squadron found itself being re-equipped with Grumman Wildcats. These F4F-3 variants were due to be sent to Greece and France but following their capitulation to German forces in 1940, the aircraft were diverted to the Royal Navy, where they were known as Martlets:

> We were flying Wildcats. We had six of these on board and they were out in the open all the time. It was a pretty rough time for the maintenance crews really. Our job was convoy protection, patrolling around the convoy quite a way out from them to see if we could spot any U-boats or, more importantly, if we could spot any of the reconnaissance aircraft that were providing the information to the U-boat 'wolf packs'. The aircraft that we were mainly concerned with was the Focke-Wulf Fw 200, which was called the 'Courier'. This was the military version of the Condor and it was an extremely well-armed aircraft that made it quite difficult to knock down. But we had quite a good amount of success against them.
>
> None of the carriers at that time were particularly fast. They weren't of the 30 knot type we have today, they were more a 14 to 17 knots type. The aircraft they were carrying didn't have high landing speeds in the main, so the arrestor wires had a limited arresting capability before they pulled the hook out or something like that. Free take-off was OK but a bad thing about landing was that whenever you landed, the aircraft that had landed before you were parked right up in the forward part of the vessel. So, between them and the landing area, two barriers were rigged. These were horizontal wire barriers that raised up from the deck on tripods. There were two of them in case you went through the first. But it was all to protect the parked aircraft up front, so the barrier was always there. It was called the safety barrier by the authorities and a crash barrier by the pilots. The crash rate into these barriers was shockingly high at that time, really shockingly high. Also, for catapulting, if you weren't doing free take-off, it was an elaborate procedure where you had to get on to a cradle and be shot off. In order to do that there were two of four huge, very heavy I would say 'blobs' on the side of the fuselage that fitted into the cradle, so you had extra weight. A very crude method of catapulting

compared with the method the Americans were using, and all together we were a bit basic in those early days. We improved rapidly as the war went on and, of course, post-war we really improved. But the crash barrier was there throughout the entire war and cost a huge number, I mean, the accident rate in the Fleet Air Arm was way above anything in the RAF. I'm talking about normal operating, not combat casualties.

The deck landing aspects prepared me for the kind of work that I was going to specialise in. What I didn't know at the time was that the captain of the *Audacity* had sent in a report to the Admiralty, he sent reports on all the pilots of course, but he had commented that I seem to have a flair for deck landing. This I think, was picked up and the next thing I found was that I was in the Navy Service Trials unit, which was mainly involved in deck landings of new types of aircraft or new types of carrier, that is to say proving the aircraft or proving the carrier.

I was sent to this job at Farnborough, where my first job was to go and land a Seafire on an escort carrier. It had already been put on a fleet carrier by the C/O of the Service Trials Unit but then I got the job of putting it on a smaller one, presumably because of my experience on *Audacity*.

It was very impressive, a first-class aeroplane for its time, and it was delightful to fly. It had no nasty characteristics at all. It was well armed. It was a potent fighting machine and it had everything that one could wish for. All I have to say, of course, it was not the best machine for work in the Fleet Air Arm because it was really not rugged enough for that sort of work. But, in spite of that, it served us very well. From then on it just grew and I stayed in test flying for the rest of my service life.

As a test pilot, Brown got to fly many versions of the Spitfire:

I have flown fourteen marks out of the various marks – and I'll tell you a very interesting little story. Once Jeffrey Quill (Vickers Supermarine chief test pilot) and I sat down together and we were discussing which was our favourite Spitfire. So, I said to him now let's not tell each other, let's get a bit of paper and scribble down our favourite mark and we both put down our favourite mark, the Mk XII, which had the Griffon engine with the clipped wings, and it was a delightful aeroplane at low level, although it wasn't terribly good at high altitude. Later marks were specifically developed for high altitude. But for pure flying exhilaration it was terrific.

The Spitfire was poor in comparison with the Focke-Wulf Fw 190 for aileron control. The 190's fault was it had a very nasty stall and if you were pulling a tight turn in combat and flicked out you were very vulnerable because you would go into a spin or you would be out of control and if you were followed down you were easy meat. So they both had this problem but provided the pilots knew their limitations I would say in a combat the result would probably be determined solely by the skill and experience of the pilot.

We realised we were primarily trying to improve the performance of British combat aircraft, so they would keep up with and hopefully exceed that what the enemy had. That was the primary purpose. The secondary purpose was to extend the flight envelope of aircraft so that we were getting into regions of high speed that we had never reached before.

The first transonic flight tests in the world were made at Farnborough in October 1941 and we were, in fact, ahead of any other nation in the world, including Germany, Italy and the United States in what we had started. The only one that kept up with this really was Germany. They had not only actually kept up with us but began to surpass us for the simple reason they had supersonic wind tunnels, which neither we nor the United States had. We were beyond a certain limit. We were feeling in the dark for the transonic speeds. As a result, we had rather a high casualty rate, fatal casualty rate mainly, in the High-Speed Flight at Farnborough.

You were, of course, aware of what you were getting into. You didn't have to do it. I've known quite a few people that opted out either before or shortly after they went into it. I found I was not in the least deterred by the high fatality rate we had. I think every one of us go through a spell in life when you feel that you're almost immortal, foolish people that we are. I was never afraid of what I was doing because I had total conviction that the boffins we were working with knew what they were up to, totally. They would take you to the limit of what they considered was a reasonable risk and I was prepared to go along with that. If they thought so, the rest was up to us. They expected a standard of skill from you but that had already been checked. So, you were in a game where things could go wrong, as they do in any form of operation. I certainly don't consider a test pilot's life as dangerous as it had been in Bomber Command. It was a different kind of risk. We had the high fatalities, that's true, but the reason it was a high fatality risk was because we were pushing the envelope all the time. We were trying to go at speeds that had never been reached before and while estimations were made and very academic estimations were made for how far we could go, we had no supersonic wind tunnels to prove the point and this was our main shortcoming so we were, up to a point, explorers.

For example, the USAAF was having problems with escort fighters like the P-47 Thunderbolt and P-38 Lightning diving down on the German fighters but failing to actually engage them. Some just went straight down into the ground. Jimmy Doolittle [USAAF Eighth Air Force Commander] came in and he came to Farnborough and he asked us to check out the P-47, the P-38 and a new aircraft that had just arrived, the P-51 [Mustang]. At Farnborough we were flying with Mach meters in the cockpit that told us exactly at what Mach number things were happening. There were no Mach meters in any combat aircraft in the entire Allied forces, none. So, there was no use telling them not to go beyond Mach so and so. We had to do the tests and note what characteristics were happening to control at these Mach numbers and then tell them not to exceed them if these handling characteristics occurred. The P-38 and P-47 failed miserably compared with the German aircraft at high Mach numbers, the P-51 was better than the Germans and so the problem was solved in that respect. But, you could tell them not to exceed a certain speed at a certain height but in combat you couldn't sit there working out the height and speed in the height of battle. You got to know what's happening in the controls, learn the controls. Have you got vibration or have you got just a bad buzz in the controls? You have got to differentiate between those things. So, that was how we explained it to them, in flight characteristics, not in terms of Mach numbers. What they wanted to know was what was the tactical Mach number, which is the number at which they could fight the aircraft. They also wanted to know the critical Mach number, which is the one that if you go beyond it, you lose control. So, these two had to be identified by flying characteristics.

In my view Britain had three top-notch aircraft throughout World War 2. They were, obviously, the Spitfire, the Mosquito and the Lancaster. They were unique I think, in our armoury. The Mosquito was truly, a great aeroplane. There was no equivalent in Germany that could match it for performance and versatility because it did a large number of roles from photographic reconnaissance down to, well not 'dam busting' here but it was going to eventually [drop 'bouncing bombs'] against capital ships in their harbours in Japan. So, there were these wonderful aeroplanes.

The Navy was interested in using the Mosquito for the very purpose I've just said: that it was going to be used with these spinning bombs against capital ships in their harbour in Japan. The aircraft, the bombs, etcetera, were eventually in Japan ready to go when the atom bomb was dropped, so it never transpired. But we never intended to use the Mosquito at sea, as a Sea Mosquito, because it had some shortcomings for deck landing. We were going to use it in Japan. The RAF were going to use it and all we were hoping for was that they would not attempt to come back to land back on once they dropped the bomb. It was really a springboard for the attack and hopefully they would land elsewhere. Nevertheless, they whetted our appetite for the possibilities of an aeroplane like this that would be very compatible with deck landing and, of course, its successor was a dream come true, the Hornet. The Hornet still remains my favourite aircraft for two simple reasons: firstly, it was one of the few aircraft I've ever flown that was totally overpowered. This is a magnificent feeling. Usually you were struggling with aircraft that were short of power, particularly when they were multi-engined. Secondly, it had beautiful harmony of control. In other words, a pilot flying a thing like this feels he's not flying, he's part of it, almost bonded in with the aircraft. You really just feel as if it is you flying it, this thing is taking you where you're pointing it and you don't have to fight it to get it there. So, that remains my favourite piston-engined aircraft.

One had to try and impress on them that now they were going to be in a slightly different world in the sense they were going to have to learn to land at speeds that they never dealt with before. Landing speed in the Pilots Notes for a Mosquito is 125mph. I was told when I landed the Mosquito on the carrier that the maximum speed I must achieve was 82mph now. So, that was below the stalling speed. So how was I to do that? Of course, you did it by using a lot of power and hanging on the props. This took a lot of trying to convince RAF pilots to do. I don't think I really did ever convince them that this was the case, so one had to do one's best and show them at least how it was achieved and they appreciated that you could lower the speed a lot by hanging on the props a bit. The other thing they had to realise was they hadn't a load of space to land on and it seemed to be as they came in to be full of obstructions. It was a psychological exercise rather than a practical training exercise, to be frank with you.

You marked out an area on the runway that was not the entire deck and I told them that was the area in which they had to arrive, and I got them to practise to arrive on that. They arrived quite often at a much higher speed than would have been acceptable on a carrier. They were given a number of (Fairey) Barracudas, which was the easiest aircraft in the world to deck land to practise on, on an actual carrier – and they broke five of those. So, the omens were not good! But, as long as we provided them with a safe landing speed, even if they crashed on the deck, they would be home.

Despite the enormous risks, the work at Farnborough was not without its lighter moments:

We had a rocket catapult at Farnborough. In effect, it was a trolley on which the aircraft was poised and at the back of the trolley were rockets. But the front had two large prongs sticking out of the trolley and as it went along these prongs penetrated two tubes that were closed, filled with water and had a disk over them so that the trolley would slow down in something like 12ft by these prongs penetrating the tubes. On one occasion everybody knew Churchill was coming to see this demonstration and it was an Irishman who was a bit excitable because Churchill was coming and in this case he failed to fill the tubes with water. He put the disks in but these were put in first and then you filled them with water. He had forgotten to do that in his excitement about the whole affair so when we went off the disks went clean through the tubes and the trolley stayed firmly attached to the aircraft. So, I was blasting full power trying to keep the aircraft airborne, going round the airfield with this large trolley hanging underneath me. Churchill was asked what he thought about it afterwards and he said it was a very impressive demonstration. He had no idea that the trolley was not meant to be there at all. The Irishman who was supposed to fill the tubes with water was called Murphy and Murphy's Law seemed to be very apt on this occasion.

A major part of our work at Farnborough was really fault finding. We had aircraft sent to us that came with known faults. There were others that came, and we found faults. To give you an example of one arriving with faults but no known faults, the Avro Tudor, the first pressurised airliner after the war, which was built by Roy Chadwick who built the magnificent Lancaster, this aircraft arrived at Farnborough with thirteen major aerodynamic faults. Now the designer was a genius previously, and then suddenly this can happen. We improved it tremendously, but we never totally cured it and it had in the end, a rather sad history. That is an example of one arriving with faults. There were others that came for example, a Typhoon. When it was flying the Sabre engine was a bit, I would say, unreliable. It was prone to not just seizing but cutting when it was flying and pick up again. But, when it cut, it cut dead. You got a tremendous torque reaction and the fuselage would swing and eventually the back ends of the fuselage were snapping off. Now, this was a design fault that hadn't been found until the engine problems arose and then it suddenly was revealed what had happened. That, of course, caused a major

28

hiatus in the Typhoon. Its ability to act as a fighter. Typhoon then really became almost exclusively concerned with ground attack. As a fighter people were frightened to manoeuvre it to that degree, knowing what could happen if you had a weak rear end, I would say, so we spent a lot of our time finding out what snags were associated with a particular aircraft.

I was totally immersed with test flying. I knew that career-wise, it was the kiss of death because you are too divorced from your service. I mean taking my career at Farnborough, to have spent six years there and never really been near the Navy except for deck-landing trials you can see that this isn't the perfect thing to have on your CV. So you realise that you are sacrificing that. But I never hesitated in feeling that it was all worthwhile because there were people I met in test flying, the excitement of it and the satisfaction of it far surpassed anything I think I would have felt in what I call the 'salt sea navy'.

Brown's fluency in German saw him assigned to one of the most unusual tasks of his test flying career. As the war progressed, Britain was accumulating a number of enemy aircraft. Some had been captured or repaired after being crash landed. One or two had even accidently landed on British airfields after their pilots had made navigational errors. Test flying them was vital to gaining an insight into how they performed:

One has to realise I was operating in different flights at Farnborough. Primarily, I was in the Naval Flight. That is to say I was mainly doing the first deck landings of new service aircraft on carriers. Then I was in the Aerodynamics Flight, which was really just improving performance generally. Then I was in the High Speed Flight, which was a very select Flight where we were really aiming ultimately at breaking the sound barrier. Then I was head of the Enemy Aircraft Flight and the reason for that mainly being I spoke German. But you may ask, 'What was the Enemy Aircraft Flight for?' It was there because there were many German aircraft shot down over the United Kingdom that crash-landed or some of them because the pilot was still alive, wounded maybe, but crash-landed so they were repairable, and we repaired them. Or, there were even some that landed by mistake at other fields thinking they were in France.

There was, to my knowledge, only one defection in the bomber side and one in the fighter side in the whole war. I don't think there were any more than those defections. So, we were flying captured aircraft by virtue of having either being able to keep them, or to get them intact from people who landed by mistake in Britain, or repair those that had crash-landed.

We were trying to find out what advances they [the Germans] had made in technology. We were startled by what we found. They were way ahead of us in general aerodynamic technology because they had supersonic wind tunnels. When we went into their research establishments, mainly Göttingen, Völkenrode and Brunswick, all in the British occupation zone, we found seven supersonic wind tunnels. These would give you airstreams of about 1.2 to 1.25, something of that order, but supersonic. But down in Bavaria the Americans found, and they invited us to see it, a wind tunnel with an airstream of Mach 4.4. Unbelievable! This had been built in 1939 by Wernher von Braun for the development of the A-4 rocket, or the V-2 as we knew it. Not only did it have an air stream of 4.4 but it had a heated airstream, which unless you heat the airstream in the supersonic work, you will get false results in wind tunnel work like that, so he was just unbelievable. That wind tunnel still exists. The Americans took it lock stock and barrel to Maryland and it exists there today. To give you an idea how far the technology advanced, the fastest Allied fighter of World War Two was the Spitfire 14 with top speed of 446mph. When I brought the Me 262 back to Farnborough and tested it we had a top speed of 568mph – 446 against 568, almost 125mph superior to our best fighter. In many ways we can be thankful that things finished as they did and when they did. But I don't think up to a point that would have mattered because the writing was on the wall for the Germans anyway because they were running short of pilots. They had no tour of duty for a pilot. A pilot was in from the beginning until he died. He was always going to be an operational pilot, so they lost a lot of people. Secondly, they were running out of fuel. We and the Americans had bombed the oil refineries in Romania out of existence, so they were going to run out of steam on both these counts. But if they had had the pilots and had the fuel, they could have prolonged the war with aircraft with the performance that they had.

We passed on what we found to technical establishments, to aircraft designers a little later, to inform people what we had found and give them access to all the data we had picked up. We actually utilised the wind tunnels we picked up. We brought them back and stored some at Farnborough and it helped us fill in a huge gap in our knowledge of high-speed flight in the very difficult phase between transonic and supersonic.

We did the odd demonstration to VIPs. We tended to limit that because we didn't want to waste the time we had on the engines. But we had a whole week of demonstrating all our captured aircraft to the public. That was in October, November 1945. We demonstrated all three jets we had. We didn't demonstrate the 163 because we were forbidden to bring concentrated hydrogen peroxide into the UK, so we couldn't demonstrate that. But we did demonstrate all three jets and that resulted in a fatal accident in one of those jets. We lost the Heinkel 162. I had been flying the Heinkel 162 during the main demonstrations and the C/O of Aero Flight had been flying the Me 262 and he got a cold on the last day so they wouldn't let him fly, so I had to fly the 262. We had a fairly new test pilot who we let fly the 162. He had flown it once or twice before but not in demonstrations, just handling. But on this demonstration he was very heavily briefed about the fact that it had a tremendously high rate of roll but a very sensitive rudder and that when he was demonstrating this high rate of roll he had to be sure he didn't try and make it even higher by ruddering at the same time. But unfortunately, he chose to do so and the tail snapped off and it went in. It had an ejection seat, but he didn't have a chance to use it.

There was no doubt about it in my mind, the Messerschmitt 262 was the most formidable aircraft of World War Two. The Arado 234B, which was a bomber/reconnaissance aircraft, had no defensive armament. It relied totally on speed and was also an outstanding aircraft but it was straight winged, not swept wing, but it was still the fastest twin-engined bomber type in the world. But the Messerschmitt was the fastest of the lot. As a fighter you didn't use the Messerschmitt for dogfighting.

You made slashes at your opposition and the tremendous fire power you had, because it had four 30mm cannon, that fire power plus the speed, you just slashed at it and vanished. This aeroplane was also a beautiful aeroplane to fly. Its flying controls and with this fantastic speed, you just felt a feeling of great supremacy when you were in it. The one drawback, and it was a serious drawback of course, was that the engines were very temperamental, I mean *very*. They really made the adrenaline flow because they had to be handled very gingerly, particularly at high altitude, but it was still a wonderful aeroplane.

In the last year of the war, Eric Brown was one of a select team of test pilots exploring high-speed flight. Piston-engine aircraft such as the P-51 Mustang and later-mark Spitfires were reaching the limits of what was possible, partly because the engine could not produce enough power but also the poor aerodynamics of piston aircraft created resistance through which the aircraft could simply not penetrate. The Germans had made great inroads into the study of aerodynamics and there was intense competition among the Allies to be the first to discover their secrets. As Allied forces swept across Western Europe, they discovered numerous secret testing establishments. With his knowledge of German language and German aircraft, Eric was sent to Germany to glean as much information as he could from these establishments:

We found three Horten IXs in various stages of build. The original Horten had crashed on its second test flight mainly due to the ineptitude of the pilot, who was not a proper test pilot. He had been given a short acquaintance with jet aircraft at Rechlin but that lasted only about two or three weeks and then he had been handed over to the Horten brothers. They used him in the Horten IX and he lost an engine in the 'Nine' and made a mess of the landing. But this was a startlingly promising aircraft, full of innovation, and its top speed was estimated by our boffins as being the same as the Me 262 with twice the range. It had twin axial-flow jets and the interesting thing is that only lately some scientists have suddenly taken an interest in this aircraft and subjected it to stealth tests and found it had superb stealth characteristics.

I interrogated most of the top designers at Focke-Wulf, Messerschmitt, Arado and Blohm und Voss, quite a few. The one that stands out is the Focke-Wulf Chief Designer, Kurt Tank, for this reason: he was not only the Chief Designer for Focke-Wulf, producing some brilliant stuff like the Focke-Wulf 190, But he was also the assistant chief test pilot. So, here you had a man who was designing, then making the first flight, often, in his own design, so he had to get it right! In my opinion he was quite brilliant. As far as I knew from talking to him, he had no political connections at all but he was a strong patriot. For example, it is known that when he was testing the Focke-Wulf 190, which turned out to be a brilliant design, after doing a test he would actually go around to see if there were any British aircraft coming along his way because he was looking for a fight – he really wanted to test out his aircraft in combat. He was that sort of guy. I said I interrogated him but frankly he interrogated me because I got few words in edgeways because he wanted to know what I thought as I flew many types of Focke-Wulf aircraft and he wanted to know in detail what I thought of each one of them and we had a bit of 'toing and froing' on this but all very amicable. He wanted to come to Britain as he knew he was near the end of his career in Germany. I think we made a mistake by not accepting Kurt Tank but we were in a phase of 'no Nazis here' and that was that.

Messerschmitt (Willy) was a very different proposition. Testy and with political connections. I don't know if he was a card-carrying Nazi but he certainly was very much associated with the upper ranks of the Nazi party. For example, there was his connection with Rudolf Hess. I tackled him about his design of the Me 109 because, although it was a good workhorse, I never thought much of it, frankly, as a fighter. It was not at all in the same category as the Focke-Wulf 190 and, indeed, in the later stages of the war there were quite a lot of reports of wings coming off the 109 in combat. I asked him what were they up to that caused the wings to come off the 109? They must have not been working to the structural limits set by the aviation ministry. He said that he had to give way a bit because Adolf Galland was always on his back about the aircraft not being up to the Spitfire. He said that Galland wanted above all to have an improved rate of climb and in order for him to get it he had to pare down on the structural integrity of the wings. He said that he could go so far and it would be fine. Obviously, they were pulling a lot more 'G' than he had anticipated or that Galland had told him. So, we had our toing and froing on that, but he wasn't delighted to be asked about that. But, generally speaking he was pretty silent. He did design the Me 262. He did not design the Me 163. Lippisch designed that. He (Messerschmitt) merely produced. This is the one thing that Messerschmitt was brilliant at and that was production. The 109 was chosen not because it was better than the Heinkel 112 but because it could be produced much easier and Hitler wanted numbers. What Messerschmitt did with the 109 was that he designed the fuselage with the undercarriage on the fuselage, and that could be built as a separate unit. The wings could be built in other places and then all brought together, which is very rare indeed for fighter aircraft construction.

The most brilliant person I met in this area, probably, was Wernher von Braun. He was not an aircraft constructor, of course, he was a rocket construction specialist. I have never met a man who exuded so much confidence. He knew exactly what he wanted and where he was going. He didn't speak much English at this stage, I met him just after he was captured but in no time at all he was fluent in English. He had such a brilliant mind and he knew exactly what he wanted to do. He told us he wanted to go to the Moon and he said he knew how to do it. Of course, everybody 'poo-pooed' it at that time but this was the man who had built the V-2, so he was not to be laughed at. The Americans were going to take him back and try him out come hell or high water because he could have been arraigned as a war criminal for using slave labour to build the A-4 rocket. But when they took him back to the States he took the majority of his very large team with him; he didn't go on his own and produced the goods. He really was 'top notch'.

Some test pilots were good but they were mainly the older ones. As the war progressed there was so much pressure put on the test pilots that a lot of them collapsed with mental breakdowns and that type of thing. The older ones were just pensioned off. Probably the best of their test pilots was at

Rechlin, called Erich Warsitz. Erich Warsitz flew a lot of the models, which were Heinkel 112 rejects because the Luftwaffe didn't employ the 112 so there were only a limited number built. They were given to von Braun to try his rockets out on and Warsitz flew all those. He had a lot of rocket explosions when he was sitting in the cockpit, one just after take-off although fortunately not a huge one. Eventually Warsitz flew the first ever jet aircraft, the Heinkel 178. So, Warsitz was the first rocket and first jet pilot in the world.

I went after him to try and get him in Berlin but Berlin was then alive with Russians and they got to him before I did and he spent ten years in captivity, so I never got to meet him face to face.

German scientists had also carved out a lead in jet engine research. Years before the outbreak of the Second World War designers had begun the search for an alternative to pistons and propellers as a source of power. As early as 1930 a young Flight Lieutenant Frank Whittle had submitted his ideas for what we now recognise as a jet engine. Unfortunately, the Air Ministry rejected his design, costing Britain a substantial lead in the development of this new technology. However, by the outbreak of war, his idea had been resurrected and orders placed for prototype airframes to carry his engine. In May 1941 the Gloster E.28/39 flew for the first time. Although it was a relatively conventional design with straight wings, within weeks it was achieving top speeds far higher than any piston-engine aircraft in service. Orders had also been placed with Glosters for a twin-engine, jet-powered aircraft called the Meteor. The Meteor first flew in March 1943 and the following year it became the Allies' first combat jet to enter service with No. 616 Squadron based at Manston. But the Germans already had a jet fighter in service, the Messerschmitt Me 262, and the Americans were not far behind. It meant an increased workload for the test pilots at Farnborough as they grappled with the new technology and aircraft designs:

I saw Frank (Whittle) first in May 1941 but I didn't know who he was. He was merely the chief proponent at Cranwell for the first flight of the first jet. But I had no idea who he was. I didn't meet him until 1944, probably March 1944. I was doing catapult trials at Farnborough and there was this, I think he was a wing commander, standing taking an interest and watching all this. When I finished he came over to me and he said that he was very interested in what was going on because he had been involved in catapult launching at a place called Felixstowe. He said that he was a test pilot there. He didn't say who he was or anything, and he didn't mention anything about jet flying or anything. But about a month or two later when I was in the Jet Flight, I had just joined it, and he appeared and he had appeared regularly at the Jet Flight. Of course, he said that we had met before and then I realised who he was. Of course, he became very much a part of my jet life.

I knew Frank for the rest of his life. I lectured with him on occasion. We attended many things together and I realised I was lucky enough to be with a real genius, an engineering genius. He was, undoubtedly, all that. He was a man who had a difficult life with the Establishment and if he had been totally recognised for what he was at an early stage this country might have had jet squadrons available to them in wartime because he knew exactly what he was doing. I always remember one of the things he said to me early when I was flying German jets a lot and German jets – or the operational jets – were all of the axial flow type, whereas Frank had gone with centrifugal flow. The Meteor and the E.28/39 were all centrifugal flow and I said to him that their engines were faster than ours and I asked him why had he gone with centrifugal? He said he wanted to give the RAF the first jets that were simple and reliable. How right he was. Simplicity you certainly had. With centrifugal flow you had one compressor, you had one combustion chamber and one turbine. With axial flow you had a number of compressors, much smaller-diameter discs, of course, similar with the turbines, which were much smaller diameter but multiple numbers. The results were: you get a much more streamlined engine with the axial-flow engine and therefore you got a higher speed but they were complex engines and they were subject to failure, particularly in the early days. Frank's first engines had an overhaul life of 100 hours, the German axial flow engines had a *scrap* life of twenty-five hours, scrap life! Adolf Galland told me that at the end of the war when he had a wing of Me 262s, he wasn't even achieving that. He said their average failure rate was at twelve and a half hours.

So, I think Frank was on the right road. Later on we changed to axial flow too but we changed after we knew a lot more about them, about manufacturing them, what metals were required that would withstand the heat stresses, etc. So, he was hounded in his early days because people did not realise that a young man like this could have such a brilliant mind.

I was in the top-secret Jet Flight at Farnborough. I joined them about April 1944 and in the stable at that time we had a Meteor and an E.28/39. I actually flew the Meteor before the E.28/39. I had just one flight in the Meteor first. We then got a Vampire, which at that time was called the Spider Crab, and then we got an Airacomet, the American jet aircraft. So, we finished up with four aircraft. We were feeling our way in the sense that we were subjecting the aircraft to all the operational things that a piston engine could do to see how it reacted. For example, would a jet engine stand up to aerobatics in the same way? Would it stand up to flying in rain in the same way? Was it more difficult to formate with a jet aircraft than a piston, all these what you might call the basics of flying; checking out that they were all applicable to a jet aircraft or were there any differences. So, once we got through those fundamentals it was then just a question of sending them to Boscombe Down and then going through the normal routine.

We had an appalling – and I mean appalling – accident rate with the Meteor Mk 1 in service – not in testing – in the service because the terrible, fundamental error was made of training the guys on single-engine approaches and landings when they rarely happened and we lost multiple numbers, quite appalling.

In the early jets, this is only in the early ones, there was a tremendous lack of acceleration. If you opened up the jet engine too quickly you would flame it out. For example, in the E.28/39 you would hold it at the end of the runway, run it up on the brakes to full power before you took off. It took fifteen seconds to go from idling to full power in those early jets. So that involved slight risks in the sense that this could happen in the air too, slow acceleration, slow deceleration. For example, if you were coming into land and you realised you weren't doing too well, you would need a bit of power and speed and you jammed the throttle open, but you would not get the power and speed, you would probably get a flame out. So it was a question of, initially, of engine and throttle handling but later on that vanished and throttle facility became almost as good as a piston-engine aircraft.

The whole scenario changed. You came from normally conducting your aviation at low and medium levels. Normal flying was up to about 15 to 20,000ft. Suddenly you had to go up into a high-altitude world because of the fuel consumption problems. So everybody suddenly became alert to high-altitude flying and you had to learn all the lessons, which were many, not just flying. There were physical lessons to be learned. How the human body behaved differently at high altitude, how things like lack of oxygen, hypoxia, affected you. All these were highlighted suddenly.

Security was huge. When you went in the morning, at the gate, irrespective of whether you had been there like I was for six years, you were searched, mainly to see if you were taking a camera in. People often say to me, 'Oh, you must have loads of wonderful photos of Farnborough.' I don't have any wonderful photos. The only photos I have were the official ones taken at Farnborough. So that was the main thing. Then, visitors coming in were always escorted. They were never left to wander around the place. The other thing was that the general level was secret but if you got into the top-secret level then, like the Jet Flight, it was even separated on the airfield on the other side of the runway from all the other activity surrounded by RAF Regiment guard dogs, etc, etc. So the security was at a very high level indeed and I have heard very little of any breaches of security there.

However, it was a chance conversation while Eric Brown was 'off base' that led to a major breakthrough in aerodynamic research:

When we were in the throes of compressibility testing, we were fumbling in the dark a bit because we theoretically guessed what was happening with the pressure waves that go ahead of an aircraft and were forming a barrier. But it was all guess work because we had no wind tunnel that would show this, so nobody had actually seen a shock wave in full scale. Now, in 1948 we made a test at Farnborough and it all happened because I was in the barber shop at Farnborough one morning and the guy in the next chair said to me, 'You are Eric Brown, aren't you?' I said yes. He then said, 'You know I'm at Farnborough too and I'm working on a thing called a shadowgraph.' And he said, 'I have hopes of filming an actual shock wave but I've been really a bit tentative about putting it to anybody in case I was laughed out of court.' So, I asked why he didn't speak to us about it, which he did, and as a result an experiment was set up in which I flew a Vampire at dusk. It had to be done at dusk for this shadowgraph to operate.

This shadowgraph was set into the side of the fuselage pointing out along one of the wings. There was a quarter of an hour in the evening when the sun is setting, before it disappears over the horizon, so you had a quarter of an hour window in which to do it and, of course, it has to be done then because the sun was so low. So, I flew it at 540mph at low level and the shadowgraph was photographing along the wing at the time. This was our very first go. We thought they'd probably need months 'playing' with us. When I came in the next day the place was agog. They had got the most magnificent picture, the first ever seen of a shock wave and in full scale. The Americans went berserk over this because it revealed a huge amount about the formation of a shock wave in transonic flight. I would think that it was probably one of the most exciting moments in testing I had.

In the years just after the war, Britain led the world in aerodynamic and jet engine research. The 'Holy Grail' was to be the first to go faster than the speed of sound – to go supersonic. The Miles Aircraft company had been invited by the Air Ministry in 1943 to develop an aircraft capable of achieving speeds of up to 1,000mph in level flight, which was more than twice the speed record at that time. It was a tremendously ambitious project undertaken in great secrecy but by 1946 Miles had begun building the first of three research aircraft now designated the M.52. As Eric Brown had already flight tested some of the features of the new aircraft, it seemed logical that he could expect to be chosen as the first pilot to go supersonic:

I was alerted that I might well be the first to fly the Miles M.52, so therefore I was taking a very close interest in it. It was a grave disappointment to us when it was cancelled. It was cancelled because, I think there were three possibilities: one was economics. It was going to be for that time a fairly expensive project and when the war ended, of course, everything and budgets were against it. I know the second thing was that the then Chief Scientist of the time, Sir Ben Lockspeiser, had an innate worry that this aeroplane might well have a disastrous flight record and he was very, very concerned about the human aspects of asking a pilot to do stuff like this. But I can assure you there was no worry on our part. We were very keen indeed to fly it but nevertheless there it was. The third thing was that there seemed to be some doubts among the scientists at headquarters that this aircraft had enough fuel to carry out a supersonic flight from beginning to end. There was a feeling it might get to the top of the climb and run out of fuel because the design was such that the fuel tanks were distributed circularly around the engine and in consequence there was not much fuel aboard.

I would have expected it not to be an easy aeroplane to fly but I would have thought with the experience we had in Aero Flight that we could have flown it successfully. I have to admit I have doubts as to whether it would have had enough fuel to carry out the whole thing, but I think it was worth the risk and we may well have solved that problem. I'm very saddened by the fact that we didn't get to be the first nation to break the sound barrier, very saddened by that – or disappointed because I think it was within our grasp.

It was a considerable setback. To begin with, the biggest setback was morale. All the people who had been working so hard in the wind tunnel and associated with it in anyway were really very badly jolted by this cancellation in 1946. I think we lost a lot of knowhow in not having an aeroplane of this capability at this particular time, particularly when the Americans were pressing on as hard as they could and the Germans had already shown us the way.

Post-war, I think that we 'rushed our fences' at the beginning, frankly. We wanted to catch up in one fell swoop and if you take an aeroplane like for example the de Havilland 108, suddenly we had jumped from the Mosquito and the Vampire to this very advanced aeroplane with tailless design, highly

40

swept wings for those days, we were talking about 45 degrees of sweep, and we believed that this aircraft would capture or recapture that world speed record with ease. Now this was a big bite to take when you consider that we were moving from the Meteor, let's say, or the Vampire and it proved, of course, to be a jump too far because it had a very, very difficult history. It was not an easy aircraft to fly and it finished up with three fatal accidents. So I think we just bit off more than we could chew to begin with and I think that experience or some of those experiences like that, slowed us up a bit and we realised we were rushing our fences a bit. Maybe we slowed up too much. The Americans, on the other hand, went at it a little bit more slowly to begin with but in most cases, they got it right. They did have their nasty aeroplanes as well at that stage, but they didn't have quite the same problems as we were having.

In the last few months of the war, Britain continued to forge ahead into the jet age. Leading the charge were men like Eric Brown. The Gloster Meteor had entered RAF service in July 1944 and now, attention turned to exploring ways in which the Royal Navy might benefit from jet power:

In early 1945 I had been in the Jet Flight for almost a year and we had four aircraft in the stable. While I was there the previous chief test pilot at Farnborough visited us. He was called Group Captain Willie Wilson and he said, 'You're doing all this testing for which the RAF is the main beneficiary of what's going on here, so why don't you think about getting an aircraft on to an aircraft carrier – a jet aircraft.' So, I said that he would have to put the thought in the heads of the 'top brass' while I thought about it from the flying point of view. Well, he did that very thing and from above came the message 'What do you think about putting jet aircraft on a carrier?' I said that it was perfectly feasible, in my opinion, certainly as an experiment at this stage. But I said, the one thing they would have to do before we went the whole hog and put it into squadron service was get an improvement on the engine acceleration and deceleration. But otherwise, I thought it feasible.

However, we only really had one choice among these four aircraft and that was the Vampire if it could be fitted with a hook. That might have been awkward because it had tail booms. They fitted a hook to the fuselage and the Vampire was a very nice aeroplane to fly but it still had the slow acceleration of the centrifugal flow engine and indeed any jet engine at that stage. But in spite of that we decided to go ahead.

We painted out an area on the runway. Did landings in that. Satisfied ourselves that the touchdown speeds were within the speeds that the arrestor hook could cope with and got on with it after that. The big thing that had to be necessary on a jet engine to land on an aircraft carrier was the installation of air brakes. The E.28/39 didn't have air brakes, so that was out as an aircraft. The Meteor had air brakes, but it was a twin and we didn't want to start with a twin. The Airacomet was a dreadfully slow aircraft, again, a twin, and had bad acceleration. The Vampire really was the only runner from our stable and it had the air brakes and the rest, so we went ahead. The trials were successful. They taught us one or two things about air brake use in deck landing, but they also confirmed that we would have to improve the acceleration.

We did the landing [HMS *Ocean*, 3 December 1945] and I was very conscious of the fact that we had this slow acceleration, which might be needed if you got too slow on the approach. Therefore, I was quite happy about it once I had practised it. But I didn't think it was fit to send out into the training schools and get everybody going on to jets with the evidence at this stage because I felt sure, and Frank Whittle felt equally sure, it was only going to take around nine months to sort this problem. So, we had a go at it and it became a bit of an interesting race in the end because the American navy was dead keen to do this for the first time. They were using a pilot I had served under at Patuxent River, so we were both in contact with each other and he was fine. They were using an aircraft with similar performance to the Vampire, but they were also having the same dreadful trouble with acceleration and deceleration and they decided they would not go ahead until they got this problem solved. So, we were nine months ahead of them in doing it and, interestingly, that was the span Frank Whittle talked about being the time required to cure this problem of acceleration. So, he was dead on in his guesswork there.

A huge amount to satisfaction was achieved by beating the Americans, of course, but that was a nice bit of friendly competition. It contributed a lot to aviation. But strangely enough the thing that contributed mainly to naval aviation, although it didn't seem to at the time, was the flexible deck. Landing the Vampire on a rubber deck didn't go on because it was logistically not cost-effective. But it was the reason we lit on the angled deck. We were thinking of how to operate the flexible deck landing and operate a catapult at the same time, which on operations happens. If the aircraft landing on a flexible deck missed the wire, it would get into the area of the catapult. So, we were thinking what could we do? The idea of the angled deck struck us not for the main carriers but for the flexible deck. Then we realised that it was a gift for all carriers. So that was a huge thing that came out of that experiment.

It just got people's grey matter moving and somebody was bound to come up with a sparky idea. At first the guy who thought of having an angle thought it wasn't practical from an engineering point of view. But fortunately he was doodling with this on a piece of paper at a meeting and sitting next to him was the head of the naval aircraft department of Farnborough, who immediately saw the engineering aspect of it as a possibility, so the two of them shared ideas and co-operated and the result was the angled deck.

The Navy's requirements were dealt with by the Directorate of Naval Air Warfare, of which I became the Deputy Director eventually and I was in the Chair when we dreamt up the Buccaneer and the Phantom for naval aviation. That's where the ideas have to start because they are responsible for putting together the requirements, projecting what we need. The next stage was for it to go to the manufacturer to build what was projected. It then had to go to Boscombe Down for acceptance testing. It would not be accepted into service without Boscombe clearing it. Farnborough did something on the side. It did all the deck landing trials associated with a new type. It was also a 'trouble seeker'. If there was any major glitch in what was happening it was sent to Farnborough to iron that out and then it went back to Boscombe again to further acceptance. So, Farnborough was a key element in a consolidated process.

I found the jet era much easier to cope with than the piston-engine era in the type of work that we were doing at Farnborough, which was mainly in the area of transonic research. There was no way a piston engine was ever going to go faster than the speed of sound and we were hurtling down hill in these piston-engine aircraft and getting some pretty shaky rides, one must say, although we had quite a few fatalities when we moved into the jet era, it all seemed to become so much simpler.

Eric 'Winkle' Brown was one of the UK's greatest pilots, who flew 487 types of aircraft from the 1930s through to the 1980s, more than anyone before and unlikely to be surpassed. As well as being the first Fleet Air Arm pilot to fly a jet, he also completed over 2,000 landings on aircraft carrier decks. But it was for his contribution to British aviation during its difficult and perilous early years that he will be chiefly remembered.

He left the Navy in 1970 and as well as many industry honours, he was appointed to Commander of the Order of the British Empire (CBE) in 1970. Eric Brown died in February 2016 aged ninety-seven. In answering the question about what made a successful pilot he replied:

I think a lack of imagination but I think you have to have an analytical mind and a fairly cool head. Come that one time you don't want to panic in an emergency, and that is not a natural instinct. I think also I would say these three qualities are probably going to do you a lot of good, assuming of course that you have the quality of being an above average pilot.

Roland 'Bee' Beamont

Most of the pilots in this book flew aircraft designed and built by the great British aircraft manufacturers. Companies like Fairey, Gloster, A.V. Roe, and so on. Wing Commander Roland Beamont forged his reputation test flying for a company that had never even built an aeroplane until after the war. But, just two types, the Canberra and Lightning, ensured English Electric's reputation and that it would go down as one of the greats in the story of British aviation.

Roland Beamont – 'Bee' as he was widely known – had an extraordinary career as a test pilot in that it spanned four 'generations' of jet flight. His test flying career began during the Second World War as a production test pilot for Hawkers. He was the first British pilot to fly supersonic, albeit while he was in the United States, and in an American-built aircraft; he then went twice the speed of sound during the English Electric P1/Lightning programme before retiring as chief test pilot on the Panavia Tornado programme.

Roland Prosper Beamont was born on 10 August 1920 and spent his early years in Chichester. Tangmere aerodrome was nearby and the young Beamont was often to be found watching the aircraft come and go. In 1926 he experienced flight for the first time when he was taken up in an Avro 504. From that point on he was smitten, spending all his pocket money on aviation books and models.

But academic study was not the young Beamont's forte and it was only after six months of private tuition that he was able to pass the all-important School Certificate before he could progress to the next stage of his career. Having scraped together enough points to pass the exam, he presented himself at No. 13 Elementary and Reserve Training School at White Waltham Airfield for ab initio flying training as a civilian. The date was 2 September, the day after the declaration of war with Germany. In order to qualify for a short service commission, pilots had to pass this course by going solo after

45

fifteen hours tuition. Roland only just managed to pass. For the next stage of his career, he was posted to No. 13 Advanced Flying Training School, at Drem in Scotland, flying Hawker Harts and then Hurricanes. On 21 October he passed out as a pilot officer graded as exceptional.

Bee's first operational posting was to No. 87 Squadron based in France, which had been sent as part of the British Expeditionary Force in November 1939. He had logged just fifteen hours of flying Hurricanes and poor weather meant that there was little prospect of getting more experience. His chances were diminished further when he was hospitalised with a high fever. Rather than risk being removed from the squadron strength, Beamont discharged himself and returned to his squadron just as things were starting to warm up. Throughout the spring of 1940, German incursions over France increased as they tested British and French defences. In March, Beamont took part in the interception of a Heinkel 111 bomber. Then, on 8 May, he scored his first 'kill' when he shot down a Dornier Do 17.

On 10 May 1940, Germany launched its 'Blitzkrieg' in Western Europe. From the north and east, German forces swarmed down through the Netherlands and France. No. 87 Squadron was in the thick of the action as it sought to stem the tide. Within weeks the squadron had to be withdrawn back to England to re-equip. By July, No. 87 was in Exeter in a night-fighting role. At this stage of the war, night fighting relied on searchlights to find and spot the target and so it was a largely fruitless and frustrating exercise. To improve matters, Beamont came up with the idea of attacking German airfields on moonlit nights. It was a tactic that bore results and Bee was successful in destroying a number of aircraft on the ground.

In May 1941 Beamont was transferred to No. 79 Squadron as flight commander. This was followed in June by the award of a Distinguished Flying Cross. However, it was in December that he got his first introduction to test flying. He had reached the end of his first operational tour and was offered the post of Leigh-Mallory's personal aide. But there was a second choice that meant he could keep flying:

> Becoming a test pilot, it just happened. I was an ordinary Royal Air Force fighter pilot. I had been in the Battle of France and the Battle of Britain on Hurricanes and when I came to the end of my first operational tour, 'P Staff', that was the postings organisation at the Air Ministry, posted me to Hawkers for test-flying duties, which was the best possible thing I could imagine happening.

I arrived at Hawkers and learned how to be a test pilot in six months' attachment there. I got the feeling for the job, in fact I became fascinated by it and so I was very happy to go back to it when the opportunity arose later.

The requirements were very simple at that time. There were no professional organisations to train test pilots like the Empire Test Pilots' School today. Pilots were chosen for flying aptitude, and interest or keenness in the job. If a chap was thought to be particularly interested in the flying side of the work and also had good hands and co-ordination, had a record as an accurate and skilful pilot, he stood a chance of being chosen for the job. I suppose that is the way that I was selected. I wouldn't have known, nobody asked me. They just sent me there.

My first experience as a test pilot at Hawkers had lasted six months and after that I was posted back to operations for another tour. That time I commanded a Typhoon squadron, which was then a very new aeroplane I had learned a little about, test flying at Hawkers. At the end of that tour of operations I was posted back for a second period to Hawkers, this time to test the development of the Typhoon, which was the Hawker Tempest. I enjoyed that very much and became more well trained in the business of test flying.

The exigencies of war were driving aircraft development hard. New threats required new solutions but aircraft designers were facing new, fundamental problems. 'Conventional' fighters were reaching the end of their performance capabilities because of poor aerodynamics. Up until the early years of the war, the solution for more speed was met by increasing the amount of power delivered by the engine so that it could drag the airframe through the sky more quickly. But by 1942 it was realised that this was not the solution for the future as aerodynamic resistance meant that the airframe simply could not go any faster. A new era in aviation design was about to begin:

At the end of 1942/beginning of '43 Hawkers had got in development the Hawker Typhoon, which was a bog-standard 2,000 horsepower fighter to replace the Hurricane. Some aspects of the Typhoon produced a shortfall in performance: it had a very thick wing that had been specified by the Air Ministry, which mitigated against the Typhoon being able to get very much faster than it was ever going to. Putting in a bigger engine was not going to make it go faster because the wing was too thick. At the same time, this thick wing reduced the performance at altitude so that above 20,000ft the Typhoon was inferior to the Spitfire and, of course, to the enemy aeroplanes.

At around about the end of '42 when I joined Hawkers, the Hawker company chief test pilot, George Bulman, and his supporters, Ken Sexsmith and Bill Humble, had started to investigate a phenomenon that was occurring with these big new fighters, which was this loss of control and very considerable buffeting and roughness that was experienced when they were diving these aeroplanes high up. It wasn't happening low down but if they tried to get these aeroplanes to dive at their limiting speeds at high altitude, they were running into control difficulties. I joined that programme and it was a very exciting experience. For example, we took a Typhoon to 30,000ft and applied full throttle and fine pitch, rolled it into a steep, nearly vertical dive. As you approached about 450mph indicated airspeed, the aeroplane started to seem as if it was riding over cobblestones – tremendous roughness, increasing noise level, a roaring noise, controls started to stiffen. The next thing was it started to roll away to the left; you would try to put opposite control on and it wouldn't work. The next thing was the nose would go down and you would pull the stick back and it wouldn't respond, and so you were rolling left and pitching down with this tremendous noise and this roughness that was subsequently described as compressibility. This is a condition where the airflow around the airframe as it approaches the speed of sound, that is the actual air travelling around the airframe, compressed and stopped flowing smoothly. It went off into what were known as shock waves, which reduced the effectiveness of the controls and altered the pitch of the aeroplane, and eventually if you persisted it would actually go out of control and you would appear to be in a fatal situation. There were quite a number of fatal accidents where the pilots got into trouble and dived into the ground.

We at Hawkers were investigating why and we did find during that period, that was established by about 1943, that if you got into this frightening lack of control right to the point where you were actually out of control, it was rolling and diving away from you despite everything you could do with it. If you stayed there and rode it down from about 15,000ft or so down to about 10,000ft the speed of the aircraft relative to the speed of sound, as it got into the thicker air, reduced and as that occurred the shock wave died down and control came back. This was known as compressibility. It was a recognised condition by the end of '43 and the designers were very, very busy trying to design the next generation of aeroplanes that would overcome this problem. But, until they did, and it wasn't really until after the war we got aeroplanes that would actually cope right through this condition, compressibility was a limitation that all the air forces had to observe and pilots had to be trained to avoid getting into it.

It must have been extremely frightening for the chaps who got into it first. My first experience – I had been briefed by Philip Lucas, who was then the chief test pilot – I knew exactly what to expect and so I recognised it. That didn't stop it being frightening but I did at least recognise what was happening.

The German experience was similar to ours. They had actually lost an Me 109 under test at their Rechlin test establishment as early as 1941 and one of the staff pilots there, a chap called Heinrich Bauvais, then took on the programme and was instructed to dive a Messerschmitt in exactly the same conditions. He recovered from the dive and came back and reported the sort of conditions I've described about the Typhoons – this was in 1941.

The Germans set about their research in a way that was very effective. By the middle of the war they had advanced very considerably in terms of aerodynamics and high speed, and they had produced a number of experimental aircraft that could get very close to the speed of sound. The first one that was of practical value was the Messerschmitt 262, which was a twin-engine fighter. That, in 1943, was streets of head of anything that the Allies had. It was being built and developed at the same time as our Meteor, but it was a far better aerodynamic concept. It was so far advanced that the Germans were able to put it into service in 1944. They misapplied it under Hitler's direct instruction; that was one of his big mistakes. But they nevertheless had an aeroplane that had they produced it in very large quantities purely for the fighter arm, they would have done enormous damage to the USAAF and its attacks on

Germany in 1944. However, Hitler – on his express orders – said that these twin-engine jets were to be called jet bombers and they were used for ground attack, which was misuse of them. By the end of 1944 the Me 262 was capable of over 500mph, which was a good 120mph faster than the average Allied fighters of the time. It was potentially a very powerful weapon. Unfortunately, I never got to fly one. After the war they evaluated the 262 and they found that it was superior in nearly every way to our Meteor and yet it had been put into service two years earlier. So, they were very well advanced.

I don't think there was any blinding revelation. I think that they studied the Germans' achievements, in fact, some of our own people from my company, English Electric, went over to Germany in the parties of the scientists to evaluate German industry and they found that what the Germans had done was to put together all the best theory, the best of knowledge, more quickly than we had. There wasn't any major breakthrough, with one possible exception that is that the Germans were the first people to use sweeping back the wings in order to delay the compressibility effect. In broad terms, sweeping back the wing will reduce the drag and it will make an aeroplane go that much faster for a given amount of power. The Germans introduced sweep back. It wasn't really a breakthrough, it was a good advance, and in post-war, of course, the rest of the aviation world took that up.

At the end of that period [at Hawkers] in 1944, I was posted for a third and final tour of operations to cover the D-Day invasion period on the Tempest that I had been testing at the factory, so that I began to get a very good feel for this particular type of aeroplane.

As well as advances in aerodynamics and jet power the Germans had been experimenting with pilotless aircraft and weapons that could fly themselves to their targets. The Vergeltungswaffe 1 ['Vengeance Weapon 1' or more commonly referred to as the V-1] was an early cruise missile. It was powered by a pulse jet motor, the distinctive noise of which led to it being called the 'Doodlebug' or 'Buzz Bomb'. Launched from northern France, the V-1s heralded a new blitz against London. Their speed and size made them difficult targets for Britain's defences. The Tempest's low-level performance made it one of the few aircraft fast enough to compete with the V-1. Under Wing Commander Beamont's command, 150 Wing quickly racked up 638 of a total of 1,846 V-1s destroyed by aircraft:

> Shooting down V-1s required no special skills beyond good fighter pilot qualities: a chap who knew how to fly his aeroplane, had a great degree of alertness – you didn't have much time in which to complete an interception on a V-1 because it was flying about as fast as your fighter could, they were almost exactly matched in speed, you had to be a good marksman, you had to be a good shot. If you could bring all those things together then it wasn't all that difficult.

By late October, 1944 the V-1 launch sites had been overrun by the advancing Allies. London was safe once again. 150 Wing resumed its role of flying armed reconnaissance missions deep into northern Europe, attacking targets of opportunity. On 12 October 1944, Beamont took off for his 492nd operational mission. He was attacking a heavily defended troop train when the radiator in his Tempest was holed by shrapnel. With no chance of making it back, he crash-landed the Tempest without injury and was taken prisoner:

> Towards the end of the war it was becoming apparent that I could actually go back to Hawkers as a civilian test pilot if I left the Air Force. I was offered this by the chief test pilot, Philip Lucas. Of course, I would have had the option of staying in the Air Force – I could apply for an extension of my service – a permanent commission. At about the time when the decision was going to be taken, I got it wrong and ended up as a prisoner of war on the other side of the Rhine.

He remained a PoW until the camp he was held in was overrun by Soviet forces in May 1945. Unfortunately, they could hardly consider themselves 'liberated' as the Russians held them for several more weeks. On his return, Beamont found that the role of deputy experimental test pilot had been filled during his incarceration but, thanks to his contact with Philip Lucas, he was able to land a test pilot's job at the Gloster Aircraft Company:

> So, after the war I came back into the Air Force, which I had thoroughly enjoyed being in, and I had the prospect of deciding which way my career should go. I had some experience as a

test pilot, which I very much enjoyed, and I equally enjoyed being in the Royal Air Force. It was a wonderful service and so I applied for a permanent commission. This was immediately after the war. In the way things went at that time with thousands of people applying for permanent commissions, bureaucracy wheels ground slowly. I was lucky to be welcomed in as a test pilot by the Gloster aircraft company. I had been there for a short time when I had an invitation from the Air Ministry to go back for induction for a permanent commission in the Royal Air Force. My wife Pat and I had a long, long discussion about this, lasting some days I think, as to whether I should resume my career in the Air Force or whether I should take up a new career in the aircraft industry. The key factor for me was that this was the beginning of the jet era, the new jets had just arrived and there was a whole new and exciting future coming up. We elected to go into the industry.

The late 1940s was a 'golden era' for the Gloster Aircraft Company. It had designed and built Britain's first experimental jet aircraft, the E.28/39. It had followed this up with the Meteor, which was the RAF's (and other air forces around the world) first jet aircraft and was the only Allied jet fighter to enter service during the Second World War:

> The comparison of the Meteor to the Tempest, you could say that I was a little disappointed when I first flew one in 1944. The Meteor was very new, it was in the very early stages of development and it could be said that it had been rushed into service for political reasons because the flying bomb battle was going on and it probably helped to be able to say that we are employing our latest jet fighter against the V-1s.
>
> When the Meteors of 616 Squadron arrived at Manston in the summer of '44 I had my wing of Tempests just down the road at Newchurch and we were being highly successful. In two months of the V-1 battle the Tempest shot down over 600 V-1s. When the Meteors arrived I thought I must find out about this. The squadron commander was a friend of mine, so I asked him if I could come over and he said that I could come over and fly anytime. So, I went over and flew a Meteor Mk 1, I think it was, at Manston.

I was quite disappointed in it because it was not a well-developed fighter airplane. It was easy to fly. The jet engines were a remarkable experience in that they were terribly smooth and, of course, there was hardly any noise. The only thing that I felt that was of any particular interest was that at full throttle you could go about 80mph faster than my Tempest, which was capable of 430mph, so this was just about the 500mph aeroplane. But, having got to that astonishing speed, you had no alternative but to throttle back and return to base and hope to get there before the fuel ran out. So, it wasn't a very flexible fighter aeroplane and I was sure I wouldn't want to be operating Meteors at that time of the war.

The early jets were to some extent a disappointment. The Meteor was always a rather heavy, cumbersome aeroplane to be a fighter. The de Havilland Vampire was a little single-engine thing and that seemed to take full advantage of the jet engine in that it was a very lively aeroplane, very aerobatic. It was a good combat fighter but it was very restricted in radius of action, very short endurance. It was also not quite as fast as a Meteor, so in that sense it was not a particularly advanced aeroplane. It wasn't until we started get swept-wing fighters that there was a real advance in fighter performance. I think that the period after the war with the development of many types of prototypes with jets didn't produce a really effective fighter aeroplane until 1947/48, when the Americans produced the North American Sabre – F-86 – and we as a country produced by the end of the '40s the Hawker Hunter. Now, those two types were great advances. They were 600mph aeroplanes. They were fully aerobatic, and they were potentially very good fighters, very good.

Britain's post-war aviation industry was moving quickly to develop new aircraft and perhaps be the first to build a truly supersonic aircraft:

I stayed with the Gloster company for a while before I applied to the English Electric Company in the north of England, where I knew they had received the contract to design and produce our country's first jet bomber – it would be one of the first jet bombers in the world for practical purposes and I applied for the job of chief test pilot as they were forming a new team. After some months, Teddy Petter, who was the chief engineer, sent for me to have an interview there and they gave me the job.

I think that I got the job because I had two things going for me. One was that I had three tours of operational experience as a fighter pilot and as a fighter leader, and secondly, I'd had two short tours as a test pilot with the Hawker company, which gave me a good insight into production testing and experimental testing. I think I probably showed an aptitude for that. When it came to the point, my new chief, Teddy Petter was asking for advice from various referees and he spoke to an old colleague of mine, Freddie Page, who at that time was his chief draughtsman and who had been a colleague of mine at Hawkers when we were jointly developing the Hawker Tempest. I think that Freddie Page said we've got plenty of engineers up here, what we want is a test pilot with operational experience – and that's how it happened.

I think that if you were looking for a chief test pilot to take charge of a new and important civil airliner you would try to find a man who had experience in the test flying field who also had experience of the development and requirements for civil airliners. In the same way, if you're looking for a man to take charge of a military development, it can help a lot if the man has got a military background. So, as far as English Electric was concerned, they wanted someone who knew and understood and had an aptitude for test flying but could look at it from an operational point of view of having actually fought combat in fighters during the war and I think that that helped in my selection, certainly.

I started off in Lancashire in 1947 as the chief test pilot of the then new design organisation of English Electric with the specific responsibility of testing the Canberra jet bomber doing its first flight and being responsible for the test programme. It became very fascinating and that's what started off my interest in the jet developments done at English Electric right up through the 1950s, '60s and '70s.

Even though the war had ended in 1945, Britain's aviation industry continued churning out new designs spurred on by new knowledge of aerodynamics and the improving performance of the jet engine. Internationally there was a race to be the first to fly faster than the speed of sound – the 'sound barrier'. Although the Gloster Meteor had been the first Allied jet to enter service and was winning many export orders as well as setting world speed records, it was never going to break the sound barrier due to its aerodynamics. In order to reach the higher speeds, an aircraft was designed by Miles Aircraft in great secrecy. The project had been commissioned in 1943 and by 1944, with the design work almost complete, Miles was given the go ahead to build three prototypes of the M.52. By now, those involved believed that they had an aircraft capable of 1,000mph in level flight. But, in February 1947 with the first prototype nearly complete, the government delivered a bombshell. The project was cancelled with immediate effect. The reason given was one of cost and the need to cut back on budgets. However, there were dark mutterings of skulduggery: that the British had caved in to pressure from the United States. Certainly, there was an agreement in place for the sharing of data on high-speed flight. But, having received drawings and data from Miles, the US decided to cancel the agreement. On 14 October 1947, Chuck Yeager flew the Bell X-1 at Mach 1, becoming the first human to fly faster than the speed of sound in level flight.

The cancellation of the M.52 programme sent shock waves through the British aircraft industry and, although he didn't know it at the time, 'Bee' Beamont would find himself at the centre of the consequences of that cancellation as well as others later in his career:

> The cancellation of the Miles M.52 project set back the steady progress and advancement that you look for in any hi-tech industry. Aviation, like any other industry, depends on not standing still on developing and searching out new ideas and advancing. By the later years of the war the government, with considerable farsightedness I think, decided that the jet engines were coming that were going to produce a quantum leap forward in available power and that there was going to be a problem in going faster than about 90 per cent of the speed of sound. It was already known that there was a considerable problem in that area and that if further advances were to be made we had to be able to conduct research into flying at or around the speed of sound.
>
> So, they contracted with some of the fighter companies for the development of subsonic fighters. They contracted

with English Electric for the first British jet bomber, which would also be subsonic, and they contracted with the Miles company – and F.G. Miles was a brilliant innovative engineer with a great reputation – they contracted with him to develop a research aircraft that would fly up to and hopefully through the speed of sound. His approach to that was to apply ordinary standard aerodynamic principles with a single jet engine in a properly shaped fuselage but with wings that were thinner than anything that had been seen before. They were sort of razor wings and if you look at the pictures of the Miles M.52 and compare them with the Bell X-1, which was a similar period, it was an American research aeroplane with a configuration that was very, very similar.

By 1947 the Miles project was already in metal. They were building the prototype and making plans for the first transonic research flying possibly in the world at that time when our government did a U-turn and announced for public consumption that it was cancelling the M.52 project on the grounds that it would be too costly but primarily too dangerous for the pilots. The government was not going to ask test pilots to fly this thing. I don't think any of the test pilots concerned were consulted over this issue. But what we all knew was that by cancelling this project we took a sudden great step back within British aviation. Other people observed that, they were going to go ahead. The Americans were going ahead like mad. We knew the French were rebuilding their industry with the usual ingenuity. They were already talking about transonic research and later the same year the Bell Corporation in America, with Chuck Yeager as their research pilot, flew the Bell X-1 at Mach 1 for the first time. There was every chance that the British would have got there first had we not cancelled that programme.

To the aviation industry the reaction was one of horror. We had reason to be quite proud of our aviation achievements. We had built some of the world's best fighters, some of the world's best bombers. At that stage, just after the war, we were charged with building a new generation of jet aeroplanes and my company was building the first jet bomber. Miles were going to do the first supersonic aeroplane. If that was successful, we didn't know who would do it, but that would lead the way to a supersonic fighter, which had got to come because as our chief, Teddy Petter, had already observed, loudly on paper and elsewhere, if anybody was going to intercept an aircraft like the Canberra that we were building, the new jet bomber, it would have to be supersonic to do it. So, this was the atmosphere. A supersonic aeroplane had to come and then the government, for its own reasons, cancelled. There was an enormous sense that we were losing the race. We were about to lead the world and now we were being restricted and held back and then, of course, within six months the Americans did it and then progressed in leaps and bounds. We lost about ten years in the development of military fighter aeroplanes because of that decision.

We were all delighted when we heard that Chuck Yeager had gone through the 'sound barrier'. But I don't think anybody was particularly amazed. I think by that time there was enough knowledge that practical supersonics could be achieved and that there was an understanding how to do it. There were two schools of thought. One was you should build an aeroplane with a very thin wing, as thin a wing as you could make it, and tailplane as well. The other one was that you should have highly swept wings. The Bell company in America selected the thin straight wing philosophy. North American, who had studied the German experience, decided that the Messerschmitt swept wing was the thing to go for. They produced with their Sabre prototype a 35-degree swept wing. That wasn't capable of supersonic speed in level flight but it could reach it in a dive and remain controllable. At that point the barrier such as it was had been pushed aside and supersonic aerodynamics had become to be understood. From then on it was a progression of a putting more power into aeroplanes and getting faster and faster. The major hold-up from transonic loss of control, compressibility, had been overcome by then.

Six to eight months after Chuck Yeager I was lucky enough to be in the States in May 1948 and while I was there it was announced that the North American Sabre prototype had just reached Mach 1 out at Muroc Air Force Base in California. I was on an exchange visit at the time on behalf of the Ministry of Aircraft Production, as it was then. I was over there to fly American jet bomber prototypes to assess them. As most of them were unserviceable, I got on to the director of RAE Farnborough, who was visiting Washington at the time, and said that I'd heard that the Sabre was on test at Muroc, why didn't we apply for a flight in that? It worked, and I went out and flew it and saw Mach 1 on the clock for the first time. I suppose I was the first British pilot to do that because George Welch, the North American pilot, was the only other pilot who had flown it at Mach 1 and Chuck Yeager was the only chap to do it in the Bell, so I suppose I was the third to do it. This was about three months before our own British efforts reached that with John Derry in the DH.108 tailless aircraft to a little bit more than Mach 1 in September of that year and that was the first all-British effort – a British pilot in a British aeroplane.

Getting to Mach 1 was a key point of interest in the development and testing area. This business of getting to Mach 1, which had been a source of frustration for so long, and actually flying an aeroplane that was easy to fly with no embarrassing roughness or buffeting and loss of control or anything like that, to actually fly it at the speed of sound, was a very exciting thing to do and I suppose I did feel quite elated after doing it.

I always had a great admiration for the Americans in the way that when they identify something that they want to do, they then just go and do it. Behind that is the greatness of the nation, great resources, but they don't hang about. When they decide that they want to do something, they'll get after it. I've always enjoyed working with the Americans, especially in the field of aviation. That time out at Muroc in 1948 was my first experience of flying with the Americans and there's always been a great mutual respect in aviation. I think in military aviation at that time they were very, very respectful of British test flying. They told me we were leading the world in test flying. We were the first people to establish a test pilot school. It was already running, and that sort of feedback came back to me talking to these American test pilots. At the same time, they were doing programmes out there that were taking them out ahead of the rest of the world. They had great pride in that but not in a domineering way. I always found them professional and they enjoyed their work enormously, and I thought to myself these guys are going to get way ahead unless we do something to catch up with them. It took us a long time, but we caught up with them in the end.

Although English Electric had not developed aircraft during the war, it played a significant role in the development of jet aircraft in its aftermath. My understanding of the situation was that during the war years under the great expansion before the war of the Duffield Scheme of aircraft factories, English Electric became a subcontractor to Handley Page for the production – not development – first of all for the Handley Page Hampden bomber, which they did quite well, and then for Handley Page Halifax four-engine bombers, which they did supremely well. They produced I don't know how many thousands of Halifax bombers to a very high standard. Many people said at the time that they were the best Halifaxes of any of the subcontractors. That gave them a good reputation for aircraft production but they didn't have a design office.

Towards the latter part of the war in 1944, a far-seeing government was saying that there is a post-war period coming. The jet engine is on the way, we're going to have to face up to how to develop our aircraft industry to cope with the emergence of the jet engine and all that means to aviation. To some extent, the Old Guard, the traditional aircraft companies that started off in the early 1900s, might be a little bit stuck in their ways. Maybe we want some innovative thinking. I think that what they did by 1944 was to start to plan to put development contracts into a number of alternative companies, so that at least one or two would produce the goods. They gave a contract to develop a single-engine jet fighter to de Havilland, the Vampire, a twin-engine jet fighter to Gloster, the Meteor, and then they had the question of a jet bomber and who was to do the jet bomber. They cast around and then for some reason a decision was made to place the contract for the jet bomber with English Electric, who didn't have a design organisation. So, the Nelsons, subsequently Lord Nelson, was tasked with forming a new design team to work within the nucleus of the very large production company at Preston and start from scratch on a new contract, B.3/45, for a post-war jet bomber. He employed with considerable insight, Teddy Petter, who was then chief designer of Westlands and had got slightly dissatisfied with his task there, to be the chief designer of the new company at Preston. Teddy Petter was given the task of headhunting all around the industry for a new design team. But the people who were likely to come out from the big established firms and secure jobs to join an unknown firm in the north to design a jet bomber that nobody had ever thought of before were not going to be the old, set in their ways, middle-aged designers looking towards their pensions. They were going to be the young guys who would have a go and take a risk. This is exactly what happened. By 1945 end early '46, English Electric's design organisation was staffed with young engineers and specialists in all of the disciplines – aerodynamics, structures and so on. The average age must have been probably under 30, it was a very young design team, and, in the process, Teddy Petter had got some of the best. I'm thinking of people like Ray Creasey, who came from Vickers. Ray turned out to be, I would say, the greatest aerodynamicist in this country of the post-war years. He was basically responsible for the successful aerodynamics of our first jet bomber, of our first fully supersonic aircraft, the P1, of its Mach 2 development, the Lightning, the Jaguar and the British side of the Tornado. He had a tremendous success and it was men of this quality that Teddy Petter employed at Preston.

Teddy Petter was brilliant. He was in the best tradition of an English eccentric, although not a typical eccentric. His eccentricity was different from some. He was a very academic sort of character, not easy to get on with – his relationships with his staff were not necessarily very good. A lot of people found him very difficult. I found him difficult only up to a point and after that it became very good. I think he was a brilliant leader of a staff, he set up that staff. He created the beginning of the greatness of English Electric. Then, being a very eccentric sort of character and having a great deal of success having established the Canberra in 1951, he said quite reasonably, his staff felt, he said to the management of English Electric, right, I want an autonomous organisation at Warton, self-accounting. I don't want to continue being accountable

to the Preston factory. It doesn't work that way. The design
organisation wants to be separate and I want to be self-
accounting. But the bosses wouldn't let him have it so he said,
all right, I'm off and he went. Luckily for the organisation,
he promoted his number two Freddy Page, later Sir Frederick
Page, to take over. Freddie Page took over in 1951 and led it
right the way through to when he retired as chairman of British
Aerospace in 1982.

Despite the arguments and politicking going on behind the scenes, the
Canberra proved to be an extremely successful aircraft:

If I go back on the comparative performance of the Canberra
and its opposition, with the Canberra in 1950 we doubled the
performance of Bomber Command, which at that time had
300mph Lincolns. The Canberra was a 600mph aeroplane.
The Lincoln's maximum operating altitude was around about
27,000ft, the Canberra had an operating altitude of 50,000ft and
a ceiling of 55,000ft, and so it was a quantum jump forward.
When the Royal Air Force, the rather unsuspecting Air Force,
started to re-equip with Canberras in 1952, they exchanged
their lumbering old Lincolns for these incredible Canberras,
which had a performance and manoeuvrability that was
superior to the fighters of the time. This was a culture shock for
Bomber Command and it was quite a problem for them. But,
in the fullness of time came the summer exercises whereby
traditionally, Bomber Command would set up attacking forces
coming in from the Low Countries to be intercepted by the
fighter defences of this country. It became very apparent that
when the Canberras came in the Meteors weren't going to get
anywhere near them. Progressively, the Canberra force was
ordered to come lower and lower and lower until the Meteors
could actually catch them, and they actually had to come down
to about 30,000ft before they could do that.

When we first took the Canberra to the US, we could see
their Sabres trying to intercept us and I got a call wanting to
know what was going on. I was told to report to the Pentagon
in the morning. So, I went down to the Pentagon into a room
full of five-star generals, who wanted to know about this

aeroplane they were considering buying. I told them all about it and they were very interested, and then they said that there seemed to have been a communications problem the previous day. I replied that there had been no problem. They then asked why I wasn't able to give my altitude on my way down from Cape Cod. I replied that that was right because, as it was a British aircraft, it was classified information. At this they went a bit silent and then asked what my altitude over New York had been. I replied 51,000ft, to which one of them said 'Gee Whizz'. That was 10,000ft higher than the Sabres could get to.

Something was being done about the fighters well before then, I'm talking about the period of '51/52 when the Canberra was introduced into the Royal Air Force but the development of an aeroplane capable of intercepting the Canberra had started substantially in 1948.

The thinking at English Electric in 1948 led directly to the subsequent developments in the fighter field and one of Teddy Petter's moves after forming the design team at Preston. He was looking around and he thought that there was more to be found out about compressibility than was actually available from the records of the various organisations that had been carrying out testing the previous five years. For instance, although the then current Meteor 4 fighter in the Royal Air Force was quite a high-speed aeroplane and its compressibility characteristics and limitations had been mapped below 30,000ft, there was a gap in knowledge about that. He said, 'I think we should find out what happens to the Meteor in compressibility at the highest altitude. We should get a read-across to what we're thinking about doing in the development of an aeroplane capable of intercepting a Canberra.' He was already starting to think in 1948 that if anybody was going to intercept a Canberra it wasn't going to be with the existing fighters, it would have to be something much faster, which would have to be supersonic.

He persuaded the Air Ministry to loan English Electric a Meteor 4 specifically for very high-altitude research. That came into my department and I did a programme of about fifty flights of diving the Meteor at the highest altitude I could get it to – get it into its loss of control area, compressibility as high as about 41,000ft. We found a lot of interesting things out there but nothing that wasn't an extrapolation of what was known before. During this process Teddy Petter started talking with his design team and included me in the discussion on what we felt about projecting the idea of a transonic fighter? The aerodynamicists under Ray Creasey said there was absolutely no problem. They said, 'We know how to do it.' Why he had such confidence at that time, I wouldn't know.

In the discussions in 1948 about the future fighter I was asked, as the chief test pilot, what I felt about the practicability of flying at supersonic speeds in intercepts and in combat. I said I didn't think there would be any problem because it was all a question of relative speeds and that the only thing we had to resolve was controllability and we had to overcome the problems of compressibility and make the aeroplane fly as accurately, smoothly and precisely at supersonic speeds as the current generation were at subsonic speed. Based on the confidence of the aerodynamicists, Petter went to the ministry and started to lobby in 1948, saying that we had to look towards a supersonic interceptor for the future. That's what's going to happen. We could do it in this country and what's more we could do it at Preston. Let's have a contract. The discussions ranged widely and I remember the Director of RAE Farnborough coming up to Warton, talking to us and us going down to Farnborough talking to them and by 1949, the government had issued contract F.23/49 for an aircraft with transonic performance and the potential for development into an operational fighter. So, it was a technology demonstrator that could become a fighter. That became the English Electric P1. We were tasked with doing it. In parallel, the Fairey company was tasked with looking at another solution to the same problem with a pure delta wing. We at English Electric had opted to go for what was then a very radical 60-degree sweep leading edge wing with a low tailplane and Fairey opted to go for a single engine and a delta wing, and that became the FD2. From where I stood there was no competition; we were going to win.

I thought the FD2 was a very clever little experimental aeroplane, but I didn't feel that it had much potential to become a fighter. There's been a lot of contentious comment from those who maintained that the French Mirage was really a Fairey Delta built without a licence. It wasn't actually. If we had gone ahead with the Fairey Delta we would have had a very fast concept of a very capable fighter aeroplane but it would have had one big disadvantage. It was a pure delta and its pitch control was by elevons, which were all along the trailing edge of the wing. At high altitude, pull the stick back to go into a turn and the aeroplane loses lift. It virtually stops. We saw that problem with deltas with the P1 and we ensured that it had a highly swept wing, a low tailplane and pitch controls by the tailplane that you pulled on to go into a tight turn – you don't lose any lift, you don't lose any performance. The P1 concept always outperformed the delta at high altitude.

I'm not aware that there was any contention with RAE over the low tailplane. What the RAE were interested in doing was at that time the T-tail was very much favoured: high fin and rudder with a tailplane put on the top of it. Our view of that was, particularly with a 60-degree swept wing, it would have been impossible to put the tailplane high enough up on the fin to keep it safely out of the down wash from the wing at high angles of attack. So, we said the safe place to put it is right down at the bottom of the fuselage and in order to make it really safe, our wing had to go high up on the fuselage to a shoulder-wing position. The RAE challenged that and said they thought that their position would have some advantages. We actually couldn't see any advantage for it at all and we went ahead and designed the P1 our way and as a safeguard the RAE arranged for a full-scale flying model of the P1 to be built for low-speed research with a single engine by Shorts, which became the Short SB.5, and that had the ability to have its tailplane fitted at the top of the fin, halfway up the fin and at the bottom of the fuselage. I took part in the test of that too.

The SB.5 was a curious, interesting thing to fly in that it was very under-powered from take-off, which was extremely lengthy. You flew it at full throttle until it was time to go home because it wasn't getting anywhere. It was very effective in proving the English Electric theory. The SB.5 showed conclusively that the high tailplane with a 60-degree swept wing was a dangerous configuration from a stability point of view and that the tailplane had to be low. From our point of view it provided a valuable little piece of development because it was known that with these sort of sweep angles the leading edge vortex at high angles of attack could adversely affect lateral control because as the vortex flowed over the wing, over the aileron, you could have variations in aileron effectiveness. The RAE had already identified this and recommended to Warton that we should have big wing fences on the P1 like the Hunter. Our aerodynamicists said, 'No thank you, fences create drag, we don't want that. We will create a pressure fence by cutting small chord-wise slots on the leading edge of the wing in areas that are needed for inward vent valves for the fuel tanks.' They put the intakes for the vent valves at the back end of these slots and the slots effectively transferred airflow up over the wing, controlling the vortex as you got to a high angle of attack. We tested this on the SB.5 and it worked like a charm. We could go from the variations in aileron effectiveness without them at high angles of attack to no variations at all with these chord-wise slots. We cut the slots in the P1 for the first flight and they remained on the Lightning for the whole of its life. It was a good little programme.

As the Cold War deepened, Britain found itself in the front line of this new threat of conflict with the Soviet Union and its allies. However, Britain did not make it easy for itself:

We were taken by surprise and were aghast at the immediate post-war government's decision to hand over to Russia a batch of Rolls-Royce Nene engines, which were advanced centrifugal flow engines. They were as advanced as anybody else's of that particular type of engine in the world, far in advance of anything that the Russians had. We knew perfectly well that the Russian state of engineering capability at that time was that they were not so good at innovative engineering but they were extremely good at making copies. Of course, they immediately put that into Russian production and it became the power plant for the MiG-15, a very, very successful jet fighter that was a great threat to the West. Extraordinary.

The first generation of jets for the Royal Air Force were the Vampire and the Meteor. The Meteor Mk 1, 2 and 3 were inadequate, underpowered and not effective fighter aeroplanes. The Meteor Mk 4 with the Derwent 5 engines considerably uprated and slightly improved aerodynamics was a better and more capable aeroplane and provided the basis for training the fighter squadrons of the Royal Air Force in the use of jet fighters. Having said that, it was never an air superiority fighter to match aeroplanes like the North American Sabre or the MiG-15. But, it was, for the late 1940s, a good step forward. It was a reliable aeroplane and it trained the Air Force to fly formation in jets and do high-speed interception and so on. The Vampire was a more agile aeroplane and still retained the good combat capability but was a very restricted radius of action aeroplane and could not really be taken seriously as a fighter. It couldn't carry very much. It had four 20mm cannon but it couldn't carry very much of an overload other than long-range tanks, so it was a fairly restricted aeroplane. I think the period from 1945 to the end of the '40s was a period that the Air Force was putting up with the new jet aeroplanes because they were jet aeroplanes, and everybody needed that sort of speed. These aeroplanes had outpaced the fastest piston engine fighters. Having said that, I think we would have been badly placed if a war had occurred at that time as I don't think they would have been found to be very effective. From the '50s onwards the Hunter came into service, which was a very, very fine subsonic fighter. The Americans had the Sabre, which was a very fine subsonic fighter, and the British started to have the Canberra, which was the world's best twin-engine jet bomber. So, it all changed the pattern from difficulties and mediocrity in the late '40s to getting to grips with the world's best aeroplanes by the 1950s.

The pace of development placed an enormous burden on the test pilots of this era:

You can appreciate that a test pilot lives with the development of an aeroplane for many years before it flies. We're studying wind tunnel tests, discussing it with the aerodynamicists, working on the control rigs, getting the fuel forces acceptable to the pilots and so on. Before the aeroplane flies you build up a very good knowledge of how it should fly. By the time it's ready to fly you should know precisely all the numbers, the take-off speeds, the structural limitations, the 'G' limitations, the probable effects of stalling and spinning. All these things have been predicted up to a point and you have a good picture in your mind of how the aeroplane should behave. You're not going out to look at a thing that is totally alien, quite new, something that has never been seen before, you don't understand it. You're looking at something that you are very, very familiar with and what you then have to do as the pilot is to see how it actually matches up to prediction. In some cases, there could be surprises but generally speaking, a large percentage of it is all predictable. Thus, going out to make the first flight in the P1, one had been there before. We had done a week of taxying to test the brakes, test the steering more importantly, to test the braking parachute and then when we finally got all those things working together I said to the team who I was working with, I think we should do a 'straight', which is short for a straight hop. We were doing it at Boscombe Down. I said it feels fine to me, we've tested it to nose wheel lift and that I would like to do a straight before we commit ourselves to flying. Let's do that next time. We then went out and did a full power run-up, accelerating to nose wheel lift, which we'd established previously, held it in nose wheel lift until it had accelerated another 10 knots. Felt it break ground, eased the stick forward, held it parallel at 5–10ft for 500 yards and then eased it down. So, we had established it broke ground comfortably. It was stable in flight and, more importantly, we had done the first landing before we had done the first flight. That was a great confidence builder as we knew how it was going to land.

So, for Flight 1, I had virtually been there before, and I was looking forward to Flight 1 with great anticipation. It all went according to plan in every technical way you can think. However, it tended to fall apart at the seams administratively. It was an interesting first flight. There was great potential, you had two great Sapphire engines producing around 20,000lb of thrust on an airframe weighing about 27,000lb, so it was a very powerful aeroplane. It felt like a racing car to fly but its control qualities as soon as it broke ground were smooth and precise as we hoped they would be because there were irreversible power controls – hydraulically operated – and we had been able to set up the feel that the pilot wanted to have on the ground and to eliminate backlash, lost movement and that sort of thing. So, the controls were smooth and the aeroplane was responding beautifully smoothly to control, so we went straight on into the schedule, which was to get up to 15,000ft and handling within a flight envelope up 2½ 'G' and 450 knots for Flight 1. We started to go to that right away. Well, about halfway round a wide circuit from Boscombe Down, I noticed that the ground below was disappearing, and the sky above was getting rather thick. In the pressures of the day a number of us including me, probably primarily me, had been less than professional in one aspect, we were so interested so enthused with the preoccupation preparing for this flight that somewhere along the line we had not been professionally decisive about the weather. It only occurred to me afterwards that, apart from looking at the sky and using my judgement as an airman and just checking with the wind direction and speed from the tower, I hadn't actually been down to the Met Office to talk about the weather. Fault number one. The Met Office hadn't bothered to get on to us as the flight test team to give us predictions of deteriorating weather, which they said after the event they knew about. Air traffic control remained totally silent about all of this.

Halfway round the first circuit when the weather started closing in, I started calling as I realised I would need radar instructions to keep me properly under control. I called, silence. I called again, total silence. By that time, I was five minutes into the flight, the ground had disappeared at 15,000ft. There was top cloud above. I was flying between layers, but I had no radar assistance. Also, I had no on-board navigation system other than a compass as this was just a prototype. I thought OK, this is where we are going to a change of mode and I called the chase aeroplane. I was supposed to have a camera chasing me, one of the company pilots, Peter Hill-Wood. I called him, no answer, so I then called Boscombe, again no answer. I thought, I'm on my own here and this was on the first flight of the most important prototype in the country at that particular time. I was presented with a situation of changing from the technicalities to how am I going to get this thing back safely if what looks like a low layer of fog has come over the airfield and there's no radar?

Airmanship came into play. I knew I had flown a specific pattern and realised I must be in the Amesbury area. If I was going to break what appeared to be low cloud without hitting Salisbury Plain, which goes up to about 700 to 800ft, I was going to have to find the Avon Valley. I was going to have to find it by braille because there was no other way of doing it.

I turned left over roughly where I thought Amesbury might be and throttled right back to very slow speed. I had forgotten that I was flying a new aeroplane by then, it just had to work, which is a measure of the quality of the aeroplane. As I turned left over Amesbury I saw a dark layer of the stratus below and I thought that looks like it might be a bit of a hole – airmanship was working full-time here! I moved over it and as I came over this darker area I could see fields and hedges just below the hole in the clouds. I saw a bend in the river, and it was the Avon and I knew where I was. I knew I had to be somewhere south of Amesbury as there was the Avon going down to the west of Boscombe Down, so all I had to do was to go roughly due south and I could follow the Avon down past Salisbury – hopefully not hitting Salisbury Cathedral if it was in cloud at the time, and break cloud somewhere over the Avon Valley. I throttled right back to between 900 to 200 knots, I suppose. You appreciate this was an aeroplane I had never flown before and I wasn't investigating how it was flying, I was just trying to find base.

I broke cloud at about 700ft that came over a bend in the Avon between Old Sarum and Salisbury. I turned left, I could hardly see Boscombe as a layer of low stratus had moved in right over the airfield and it was down to a 200ft base. And so, I clambered back into the Boscombe circuit in this brand-new aeroplane below 200ft with a drizzle of rain on the windscreen. I could see I was in the circuit and everything was fine. I had made no radio contact and so I flew around the circuit, waggled my wings to indicate that I wanted to land home and started to set up a practice approach to see how it behaved with the undercarriage down and flaps down, always supposing that these items would work because I hadn't tried them up to that point. I was supposed to have done all that at 15,000ft. It all worked fine and I found myself flying around the circuit in very poor visibility, very low in this brand new aeroplane that was flying as if I had been flying it for fifty hours. It all came to hand. It was a magnificent aeroplane. I set it up for the approach in the drizzle, lined it up and thought I would overshoot if I didn't get it right. But it felt so right I just went in and landed it first time and it was absolutely a superb handling aeroplane.

When we had a debriefing, it became apparent that another thing that I had actually asked for but had been denied was what we called a discrete frequency on which I, the chase aeroplane and Boscombe Down could communicate between each other with no other chatter on it. This had been denied. What had happened was that after I took off, the first time I called Boscombe, they had gone on to the frequency that they were talking to the chase aircraft on so I couldn't talk to Boscombe and I couldn't hear them talking. Then, they realised that there was something happening, so they switched on to my frequency, by which time I had changed frequency to the airfield guard to see if I could raise one of them. As a result, the chase aeroplane, myself and Boscombe Down spent the whole of that flight changing frequencies and not talking to each other. We all learnt from that.

On the second flight we took it up to 30,000ft, which was pretty good progress, and we then put it up to the maximum speed it was cleared for flight resonance, which was 450 knots, and that produced a 0.98 Mach number. It was already transonic, it was getting right up there. There were no problems at all, it was flying beautifully. I came back, discussed it all, I had identified one or two items that needed further investigation, but it was all flying beautifully. It felt like a really well-developed, high-quality fighter.

In debriefing afterwards the engineers sucked their teeth a bit and said that they must reduce the record, in those days it took them a few hours to reduce the tapes and to study them and find out what was going on. These days you get immediate feedback and read out from air-to-ground transmission and the engineers are actually seeing what's happening on the ground while you're doing the test. In those days it probably took half a day to reduce the records.

After a few hours Don Horsfield phoned me up, I was at the pub, and he said that the trip I'd done in the morning I'd been transonic at about 0.97 indicated. When that was factored up it was actually Mach 1. I said I wasn't sure as there had been no jump up on the static system. He said that's right, but you were just about at Mach one. Next time you'll go through.

The next flight was Flight 3 and we planned it as a normal professional plan to take it up to 40,000ft, accelerate to 450 knots and see what happened on the Mach meter. Somewhere around about Selsey Bill going up the Channel on a bright sunny day, the Mach meter went up to where it had before, hesitated there for a very short time, then swung up to 1.02. We were supersonic. I took my hands off the stick and my feet off the rudder bar and the aeroplane stayed absolutely firm, no trim displacement or anything like that, small control inputs left stick, right stick, pitch up and down, smooth, stable responses and we had a supersonic aeroplane. No vibration, buffet, nothing at all. That was a good feeling.

We had very few fundamental problems. The design offices would probably say that in the evaluation and development of the P1 we had no real problems at all. We had some serviceability or reliability problems. The P1 was used as a basic research tool for the development of the Lightning. We all knew the Lightning was going to go ahead and, in fact, the Air Ministry had contracted for a production run of Lightnings off the drawing board without having a prototype. With the P1 we were looking at the stability and control supersonic speeds specifically. We could only get to Mach 1.2 with the initial engines. We needed reheat thrust to get any faster. We couldn't put variable reheat in as it was not a practical proposition. But the Armstrong Siddeley people came up with a very clever interim fixed nozzle reheat device. You couldn't open and close the nozzles so, when you were committed to having that as a reheat system, you lost a significant amount of dry thrust, which wasn't very nice as it meant you had a non-single engine safety recovery. Every flight had to be on an energy management system assuming you had shut down one engine, you would do a power glide home on the other. But with this fixed on the reheat system we eventually achieved Mach 1.53 and from 1.4 onwards we started to measure reduction in directional stability to a point where at 1.5 I said, 'That's about it, we don't need to go any further, thank you.'

The engineers had sucked their teeth and scribbled with their pencils and they said they would like to go a little bit further, just a little bit more, and that there was more thrust available. So, I took it to 1.53 on the next fight and the measured directional stability value, which was almost zero. It almost prepared to go sideways, so I said, 'That's as far as we go.' That provided the exact information they wanted to establish the increase in fin size, which we would need to stabilise the aeroplane directionally for the Lightning. That was really the most valuable contribution that aeroplane made to the programme apart from demonstrating the stability and control characteristics of this 60-degree swept wing and the low tailplane, which proved absolutely fine.

Such was the pace of development that no sooner had Mach 1 been achieved that people began to look at the possibility of speeds up to Mach 2:

At twice the speed of sound there is no marked difference between being just under or just over it. A very interesting occasion the first time; we had been flying for a year at speeds up to 1.7, 1.8 of the speed of sound. The target was to take this aeroplane to Mach 2. It wasn't a requirement for the Air Force, their requirement was for an interceptor capable of Mach 1.7. But we knew this Lightning was capable of much, much more. So there came a point when we were going to investigate it. We realised there were two possible hazard areas. One was that the intake might result in surge, which could be disruptive and even cause a lot of damage to the engine, and the other was the temperature rise around the canopy might have some temperature stress on the Perspex, on the transparencies and also have adverse effects on the cooling systems of the aircraft. These things were in minds when we took it in stages in November 1958. We took it in stages from Mach 1.9, 1.95, 1.98 and we were just under Mach 2 and then, of course, the final thing was to get it there.

Then, of course, Mach 2 was a classic target. Everybody was trying to get to Mach 2 in the aviation world at that time. The French were trying to get there. The Americans had been there for a long time but this was our point of getting back to where the Americans were with a military aeroplane. We were barrelling up the Irish Sea one day, on a brilliant clear day keeping well clear of Douglas, Isle of Man, on one side and Sellafield on the right to keep the supersonic boom away from the coastlines as far as we could. You couldn't guarantee that it wouldn't make a boom over the land but we tried, But, when we got up to around 98 per cent we knew we were just about to get to Mach 2 and that was a jolly interesting occasion because it was a target and also that the aeroplane was behaving just as it had been even when it was subsonic. It was quiet, it was smooth, it was responsive. You were looking for any errors or discrepancies. Engine instruments were fine, temperatures were within limits and then we got to Mach 2. It was almost an anticlimax because there was Mach 2 on the gauge and nothing else was happening. But then there were tests to perform again, which could be interesting because you had to establish if the aeroplane was still stable directionally where it might be starting to get difficult. That was positive. Then we were running out of fuel, so it was haul back the power and turn it back to base. We were descending on this lovely clear day over the Lake District having gone right round Dumfries and then Windermere in this supersonic turn. We were then subsonic and coming back to base with Britain's first Mach 2 aeroplane. It was a good flight.

When I got back there was nobody there! You know what the Brits are like! However, on the way home, over the radio I told them to tell Mr Page, who was the boss, that he might like to attend the briefing and he did.

In the beginning the P1 had a lot of systems that needed development. The Rolls-Royce RA.24 engines were superb engines but the reheat system was unreliable. It took three years to get that reliability right. That was an embarrassment in display flying as you started a loop from low level, bang in the reheat and you would find yourself without enough thrust to complete the manoeuvre! So, three years to get that right. Then, there were lots of development problems with the fuel system, the starting system, the hydraulic system, and this did start to give the Lightning a bad name in the engineering branch of the Air Force. You had this aircraft coming into service that was going to give them an awful lot of engineering problems and in fact it did. They were unable to cope with them very well and there's no doubt that the engineers tended to lose their faith in the Lightning. From their point of view, it was too much of a maintenance problem. That was a counterbalance for the euphoria the fighter pilots had. The fighter pilots all loved it but by the mid-1960s there was a lowering of morale in the Air Force about the Lightning and there was talk of needing to replace it. It was a misjudgement I think but that's how it happened.

Eventually the Lightning's reliability was sorted out but it could have been sorted out much earlier with positive support from the Ministry. We had modification programmes for certain parts of the aircraft's systems starting well in the '60s that were delayed for years, and so the Lightning in service went on having these troubles. But, as a basic operating aeroplane, once the weapon system and the AI.23 radar had been brought up to standard then it became a very good operational aeroplane within its limitations. Its limitations were that it was a short-range interceptor. Again, in my view, a very erroneous specification in the early days, when we were told that this aeroplane had to be designed round a radius of action of 150 nautical miles from the V Bomber bases and its main task was only to defend those bases. This limited the aeroplane enormously and actually after the first flight of the Lightning I wrote a very positive handling report and I concluded it by saying, however, despite all that's gone before, we will never stand a chance of exporting this Lightning anywhere around the world until we double the internal fuel capacity and six years later it was done, but very tardily.

It was no problem to increase the endurance. We had a small ventral tank in the back that the aerodynamicists very cleverly found that they could extend within the area rule, which was the way of insuring against increased supersonic drag. They could extend that to almost double the capacity of the tank. That was done for the Mk 6.

There was a fire risk during the first two or three years due the integrity of the engine exhaust system. You had two very big hot engines very close together in the fuselage, the jet pipe systems, the proximity of high-pressure hydraulic pipelines, and leaks of the hydraulics or fractures of hydraulic pipes could produce fine sprays of hydraulic oil. That in turn didn't actually flame but it was charring around everywhere, and this used to set off the fire warnings. So, in the first two or three years of Lightning testing it was almost the norm to come back with a fire warning on. But eventually the fire integrity was improved to a satisfactory standard.

It was two or three rather bad years and my deputy and colleague, Jimmy Dell, had a near tragedy. He had what we called a mandatory fire warning on one day and called that he was coming back with this fire warning. On the approach on the last 100 yards or so he almost lost aileron control and on touch-down as he pulled the stick back it stayed solid. He couldn't move the aeroplane, so he called for assistance, to bring a ladder out. When the fire brigade came out they found a great big fire burning in the side of the fuselage. He had come back with a hydraulic fire burning all the way. Another thirty seconds and he would have gone in.

For the first year or two when it [the Lightning] was all new, everybody was learning about it and I think the pilots were being asked an immense task to operate that whole weapon system in adverse weather conditions and at night. I think that they did some very courageous work. There were some losses, particularly during low-level intercepts at night over the North Sea and that sort of thing. As they got to understand the system, the reliability improved, particularly the radar's reliability improved.

You must appreciate that because of the lowering of morale, the Ministry said they were going to phase out the Lightning after six or seven years. In fact, they kept it in service for twenty-seven years and by the fifteenth to the twentieth year it was working like a charm and the pilots were happy with their work and were able to cope. It was then being said that the single-pilot operation of an all-weather weapon system like this is in fact, practical. But one time they were saying it's not and we will have to go back to two seats. Well, that's gone to and fro. The Phantom was a two-seater, largely because of the argument that it needed two crew to operate in all weathers. The Tornado F3 was a two-seater. Now you have the EF2000 (Eurofighter), which is a single-seater, to do a far more complex job albeit with much more capable equipment. So, the answer is the scale of effort required has to be kept down to the capabilities of the human pilot. At one stage with the Lightning it looked as if we had gone too far. But by halfway through the Lightning's career it had come back and it was alright.

During the 1950s and '60s there was a huge expansion of air shows around the world. Events like the Society of British Aircraft (later Aerospace) Constructors or SBAC show at Farnborough used to draw hundreds of thousands of people to see the latest aircraft perform. The event not only provided a 'shop window' for aircraft manufacturers to promote their products to foreign buyers but was also a chance for them to also entertain the public whose taxes helped fund defence budgets. Many of the test pilots who flew the displays became household names, Roland 'Bee' Beamont among them:

Display flying is a different branch of activity. Aerobatic flying is always fun. Nice display flying, if it's going to be done properly, has to be practised, and that's a problem as you have got to get the time to do the practice. There was at one time a division of opinion among pilots as to whether you got the best displays by practising a routine and sticking to it or by improvising. The great improvisers of the past, when you compare them, were never as good as the chaps who practised a routine and got it right. There's a great deal of satisfaction in working up a routine in a high-performance aeroplane and performing it correctly. There are so many factors that can get in the way: You can start off, taxy out and there's a clear blue sky above and the chap ahead of you is doing his performance and doing it very well and all of a sudden the sun goes in. You

76

look over your shoulder and there is a bank of cloud coming up and by the time you roll out on to the runway numbers to start your show, you've got a 2,000ft cloud base instead of an infinite sky and you've got to alter your programme accordingly. Those sorts of frustrations occur. Flying aerobatics in the P1 and in the Lightning was always a delight because you had an enormous power to weight ratio combined with the most superb controllability. The English Electric design team knew in designing the country's first twice the speed of sound aeroplane, the Mach 2 Lightning, that they had to have control qualities that were better than anything that had gone before because the pilot was going to have to cope with twice the speed of the other subsonic fighters like the Hunter. We did actually succeed. We had the most beautiful flying control qualities; precision control was marvellous. You could place a Lightning anywhere you wanted to in the sky. Coupled with that, or at least partly because of it, you had a power to weight ratio that on the Lightning, with no military load that is, no bombs or guns and ammunition and just basic internal fuel, had 30,000lb-plus of thrust on a 29,000lb aeroplane, which meant that if you pulled the stick back on take-off at the right speed to go vertical, you went on up vertically. Of course, the Royal Air Force did that with enormous panache in the early 1960s with 74 Squadron. They started off their demonstrations by vertical climbing up to the cloud base, which was always good fun. The Lightning always had excess of power, complete controllability and the pilot could really make it 'talk'. It was a lovely experience; I always loved flying the Lightning.

The contract to export Lightnings to Saudi Arabia was vitally important to the future of the export potential of this country. We had just suffered the traumatic experience of the cancellation of TSR2. The factory was left in a state of shock, offloading staff. Hundreds were made redundant, which is a very nasty experience both for the people who are doing it and the people that are left. There was the question of how to provide the work to keep the factory floor occupied, provide the load for the drawing office and all the rest of it. We had lost our main future project. There was nothing else actually coming along. The design office very quickly got into action with the first international programme, the Anglo-French Jaguar. That occupied them almost immediately. But how to occupy the factory? The Lightning was phasing out, production was ending in '67/68. TSR2 was not going to be built but what was going to happen? Exports, if we could obtain them, were of tremendous value. But nobody realised how valuable that was going to be.

Under Freddy Page a massive effort was put forward trying to get into Saudi Arabia. We knew the Saudis wanted to make their air defences supersonic. The Americans were in there in 'task force', they were determined to win this contract. We had people out there working very hard and we were able to persuade the Saudis that they should look at the Lightning.

I don't know how much encouragement we got from the British Government, I doubt if we got any at all. But what we had to do was to explain to the Saudis that if they bought a Lightning with all its enormous capability, it wouldn't be the Lightning that the Air Force was restricted with, which was the Mk 6, but that it would have additional capabilities of up to supersonic speed: reconnaissance, under-wing stores – rockets or bombs, 2in rockets – it was a multi-role aeroplane, and over-wing tanks as well. We had done all of these things separately and now we were going to bring them all together, except for the Vinten camera pod, if the Saudis wanted it.

They came over and did an evaluation. They said they would not entertain thoughts of having our aeroplane until their test pilot tested it. They sent their test pilot down and said he will fly your Lightning. We said OK, fine, what experience had he had? They replied that he was current on Sabres. I said that would be alright to convert following some dual. They then said that there would be no time for that. The Saudi authorities said he will do one dual flight and one solo flight and during that flight, his first flight in a Lightning, he must go to Mach 2. This was a chap who was going to make his first flight in a Lightning and go to Mach 2! It was the sort of thing that would throw the Lightning Conversion Unit at Coltishall into complete disarray! Anyway, he came over and did this and it was really quite exciting because again my colleague Jimmy Dell was going to fly chase to be with him, to be there to help him.

I went into the tower to monitor what was going on. Halfway through the sortie Jimmy Dell's voice came on as I had called him to ask how things were going and he said, 'I don't know, I can't see him.' I thought, 'Oh my God, what's happened now?' He said 'he's way ahead of me but I'm going to try and cut him off,' and I thought, 'What on earth has gone wrong here?' They came back in and landed. Just before the debriefing I asked Jim what had happened? I had given Jim the latest development of the Lightning, the Mk 3, which was supposed to be faster and more powerful than the Mk 2 that the Saudi test pilot was flying for obvious reasons – to keep him in touch. Jim said that he couldn't keep up with him, that once he got to Mach 2 he realised that the Saudi pilot was going much faster than him and so he had hollered at him to turn to starboard so that he could cut him off. In the debrief, the Saudi test pilot talked about his flying quite eloquently and when he got to the end of his supersonic run he said, 'You British are honest. Your fighter will go faster than you say it will.' He had actually flown it to about Mach 2.1, which was faster than we had tested it!

After that it was tested in Riyadh. The Saudis then gave us a contract to produce 'X' number of Lightnings for their forces, I think it was something around sixty, with jet trainers to train the air force and administration and ground support. That was the start of the contract in 1965 called Magic Carpet. RAF pilots would have liked some of the lighter Saudi Lightnings as they would have been better for aerobatics. The Saudi Lightnings, the Mk 55s and 53s, were the most capable aeroplanes with the most facilities on them. They were still extremely good aeroplanes.

There was no difference in top speed between the different marks. The first Lightning I took to Mach 2 in 1958 was at the time capable of about absolute thrust equals drag at Mach 2.15. That's the highest speed that we ever had a Lightning go and that was probably its maximum. In terms of altitude, they would all do an energy climb to about 75,000ft with full reheat. So, the whole range of Lightnings, which ran into seven marks, all had the same sort of performance. They just varied in their military equipment.

I think the first prototype was my favourite because it had no weight in it. It was all power and no weight. It was a boy's aeroplane! Marvellous.

I think its power is summarised by the famous Johnny Howe's squadron, 74, when he was interviewed after his first flight in a Lightning and he was asked, 'How did you get on with your first trip in the Lightning,' and he said, 'Super, I was with it all the way until I let the brakes off.'

As the chap in charge at the factory it became my responsibility to phase the Lightning into service and that meant training the initial pilots who were going to fly. There was a little talk about this and it was quite apparent that there weren't going to be two-seater Lightnings, the T.4, until about two years after the Air Force was starting with the single-seaters. This happens time and time again for the introduction of aeroplanes. They never order the two-seater first, I don't know why. I had already established with chaps like Jimmy Dell that anybody with experience of the Hunter or a Sabre would have no difficulty with coping with the dynamics of a Lightning.

What we had to do was to train the chaps in understanding the systems, give them a good briefing and then monitor them on the radio with a Lightning pilot to talk to them if they ran into any trouble. This worked like a charm. We trained, first of all, the Boscombe pilots who were going to fly the Lightning. I think I went down and checked them out on the Lightning at Boscombe. I took a Lightning down there and showed them how to fly it and stayed with them while they flew it. Then we got six Fighter Command pilots, probably from No. 74 Squadron, and we gave them two days of systems briefings, checked them out on the Lightning – one or two flights and that was it.

There was no difficulty in transitioning from a Hunter to a Lightning in spite of the fact that it was twice as fast, which is an indication of the simplicity and general ease of flying the aeroplane. The only thing was it was a more dense aeroplane and its systems had to be well understood.

I have to say that the cockpit wasn't awfully good. We haven't been good at fighter cockpits in this country. The word 'ergonomics' hadn't been invented when we designed cockpits in the '50s and '60s. But, having said that, we were very much at the behest of the various committees in the ministries who used to tell us where to put things. We would put something 'there' and they would say, 'We don't like it, put it there,' and that would mean that something else would have to get moved. After a couple of years of this you would have a hodgepodge. So I would say don't blame the manufacturers entirely.

You can see a lot of the Lightning's features in many of today's fighters: swept wings and low tailplane – they've all got them. The exotic Russians, the F-16, F-15; they all have swept wings and low tailplanes. That is the legacy of the Lightning and that's the way they'll always be unless you go to a pure delta. These days they have overcome the delta's high-altitude manoeuvrability problem by having a foreplane pitch control, a canard in front.

If there is one thing that I would like to have seen done differently it would be twice as much fuel at the start and then end up with three times as much fuel. The fuel was the Achilles heel of the Lightning. That and some aspects of systems engineering and reliability.

The introduction of the flight refuelling probe could be a problem. For example, I broke the head off my probe the first time I used it. It's a technique, it's a skill that is learnt. It's a rapid learning curve. The first few times a chap goes up on to a tanker and tries to push the probe into the drogue – we have a drogue system in this country, the Americans have a flying boom that the tanker operator works on, we have the probe and it's a technique – I think after the second sortie you probably get it right. Nevertheless, there has to be a moment of worry if you're halfway between this country, the UK, and 700 miles south of Greenland in icy cloud at night trying to get the probe into the drogue under the floodlights of the tanker, and so on. You know you haven't got enough fuel to make a diversion. That must be a moment of some apprehension. Incidences of failure are very few. It's a pretty solid technique but it's still got an element of chance in it.

When I first saw the probe mocked up at Warton, I couldn't believe what I was seeing. This was one of the few occasions where there hadn't been direct co-ordination between the design department and the flight department. Normally, on all flying matters there was an exchange of views. I looked at this thing from the cockpit of the mock-up and the probe head was behind my shoulder. I thought, 'How in the hell am I going to steer that into a drogue that is coming down from the tanker.' I pointed this out to the designers, and they said that no one had objected before, so I said that I'm objecting now. Their response was to say too late; they had already issued the drawings, so I said that they were going to have to change the drawings then. We had a hell of a row about it but eventually we got it extended forward so that you could see the probe head in the windscreen where it ought to be. That was one of the occasions when the chief test pilot made himself unpopular!

I don't think I can think of one particular memory of flying the Lightning. It was all so enjoyable. I had fourteen years in charge of Lightning development and flying Lightnings regularly. I enjoyed every minute of it. It was a wonderful aeroplane to fly and I enjoyed the evolution of the aeroplane, and I particularly enjoyed the reaction of the fighter pilots of the Air Force to it. Everywhere I went I was the most favourite chap because I produced an aeroplane that they loved flying. It was a marvellous experience. But I will mention one single feature. For the last ten years I was a member of the Board at Warton but for a number of years of that I retained my flying category and I used to fly production line Lightnings. I wasn't doing experimental flying, Jimmy Dell was doing it by then, and every so often in a board meeting somebody would come in and whisper my ear, 'Number so and so is ready for flight,' and if the subject under discussion wasn't in my area, I'd say to the chairman, who was Freddie Page, to excuse me as I had an aeroplane to fly. He would smile and say that you can't delay an aircraft flight. I would then strap a Lightning to my back and shoot out of a smokey boardroom into 40,000ft of clear air. That was an experience I shall never forget and forty minutes later after a lovely Lightning flight doing all the things I had to I'd land it, it go back to my office, pull off my overalls, straighten my tie and go back into the boardroom, and they would probably still be talking about the same subject.

The Lightning was the last aircraft to bear the English Electric name. By the mid-1950s, Britain had too many aircraft companies chasing fewer orders as aircraft became increasingly more complex and expensive. In 1955 the Ministry of Supply began work with English Electric to develop a new low-level strike aircraft with a nuclear weapon capability. The result was the TSR2, or 'Tactical Strike and Reconnaissance 2'. Given the project's complexity and cost, English Electric were forced to merge with Vickers-Armstrong as well as the Bristol Aircraft Company and Hunting to form the British Aircraft Corporation, or BAC as it was more commonly known. However, what was meant to be a technological 'tour de force' descended into late delivery, compromise on the technologies and a vast overspend of its original budget. Eventually, on 27 September 1964, Roland Beamont, as chief test pilot, taxied TSR2 out for its first flight. There were still unresolved problems with the twin Bristol Olympus engines and the undercarriage was also proving problematic. Given these problems, it was down to Beamont to make the final call as to whether he considered the aircraft safe enough to fly. He was acutely aware of the political pressures and the aircraft was already nearly a year behind schedule. Despite these problems he decided to go ahead with a short flight, albeit with the undercarriage down.

It was not until its tenth flight that Beamont managed to fully retract the undercarriage, although there was still a violent vibration while coming into land, something that persisted throughout the flight programme.

Test flight fourteen was a milestone in the short history of the TSR2 when it went just over Mach 1 for the first time. While transiting from Boscombe Down to BAC Warton, Beamont lit a single reheat unit – there were problems with the other engine. He immediately accelerated away from the Lightning chase aircraft flown by Wing Commander Jimmy Dell. He had to use reheat on both engines to catch up!

In total, there were twenty-four TSR2 test flights over six months but there were political machinations churning away in the background. As a result, on 1 April 1965, the decision was taken to cancel the project. Cost overruns was the reason given by the government of the day but in the background were inter-service squabbles and a government that believed that missiles were the future. The optimism with which British aviation had entered the jet age was in danger of being snuffed out. Roland Beamont had seen it all first hand:

For about three years after the Duncan Sandys White Paper had been published we were concerned, yes, but those of us who had been there before thought it was full circle, here we go again. The government pulled the rug out from under the Miles M.52 in 1947, now they were pulling the rug out from under supersonic development in 1957. There was frustration, anger and, of course, concern that there might be knock-on effects from this and they might cut back the Lightning programme. But what we were more concerned about was that at that time we were interested in the future beyond the Lightning. We thought we were going to do something better and what we intended to do, given half a chance, was a supersonic replacement for the Canberra, later called TSR2. That was a worry. But we actually got a reversal of policy. We got to build the aeroplane, we got it flying beautifully and then they pulled the rug out from under that. That is the history of British aviation since World War Two.

So they then made the next cock-up. They ordered a small fleet of Phantoms and said, 'Ah, yes, we will spread the load across the industry of this country and provide jobs and employment by re-engining the Phantom with Rolls-Royce engines.' The Phantom was a very good aeroplane with its American engines. It didn't need re-engining. Putting the Rolls-Royce engines into it cost twice as much as if they had bought the American-engined Phantom and they ended up with an aeroplane that was slower than the original. I could go on!

The cancellation of TSR2 also brought the curtain down on Beamont's prototype flying career. However, as the newly appointed director of flight operations at BAC Warton, the role enabled him to continue test flying production Lightnings, which he continued to do until 1968 when he retired from test flying all together. By then he had logged more than 1,000 supersonic flights.

In 1971 Beamont was appointed flight operations director for Panavia, the consortium created to design and build the Tornado. The Tornado was designed to perform as both a fighter and bomber with variable-wing geometry. Its flexibility meant that Tornado was able to fill roles performed by several different aircraft types. However, an added complication was that Tornado had to meet the requirements of its three initial backers of Italy, Germany and the United Kingdom.

Beamont's role was to manage the flight testing for the Tornado after its first flight on 14 August 1974. The development of such a complex aircraft was not without its problems, made even more difficult by the sometimes fractious relationships between the three partners. But, on 10 July 1979, the first production Tornado made its maiden flight. Not long after, Roland Beamont announced his retirement after forty years that had seen aviation develop from subsonic piston-engine aircraft to supersonic jet aircraft capable of flying at twice the speed of sound. During his career, Beamont flew 167 different aircraft types, amassing over 5,000 hours across 8,000 flights. Roland Beamont died on 19 November 2001 aged eighty-one.

Richard 'Dickie' Martin

Richard 'Dickie' Martin was born in Bournemouth on 26 July 1918. After schooling in Cheltenham, he went to the RAF College, Cranwell, where he passed out as the best pilot of his year in August 1939. Within weeks he was posted to No. 73 Squadron to fly Hurricanes. The squadron had been posted to France after the declaration of war to fly patrols and intercept any lone bombers and reconnaissance aircraft.

It was while flying a sortie during this period often known as the Phoney War that his oxygen failed and he fainted at 21,000ft. Luckily he recovered just in time to make a forced landing in neutral Luxembourg, where he was interned. It was while he was out on his daily exercise one foggy morning that he was able to slip away, re-joining his squadron on Boxing Day 1939.

As activity increased over northern France during the spring of 1940, Dickie Martin scored his first probable success when he shot down a Messerschmitt Bf 110. It was a foretaste of what was to come as, following the launch of the Blitzkrieg on 10 May, No. 73 Squadron was constantly on the move and engaging the enemy. More successes followed until he returned to England in June following the evacuation at Dunkirk.

Although still only a junior officer, he was awarded the DFC and appointed as an instructor. At the end of that tour he re-joined No. 73 in Tobruk just as Rommel began his attack to try and drive the British and Commonwealth forces out of North Africa for good. The fighting was intense as the squadrons of the Western Desert Air Force were heavily outnumbered by the combined German and Italian air forces. Dickie was in action straightaway and scored several more 'kills' before being shot down while intercepting a raid of sixty enemy aircraft. Despite being wounded, he managed to bail out.

Once he had recovered from his wounds, Dickie was sent as a flight commander on No. 250 Squadron flying Curtiss P-40 Tomahawks.

In 1943 he returned to England and the following year converted to flying Dakotas before being sent to India to join No. 52 Squadron. He was soon flying supplies and mail over the Himalayas, known as the notorious 'Hump route'. It was while he was in India that Dickie Martin's career changed direction:

> I was flying Dakotas in India when they decided they would post me back to the UK on a test pilots' course. I think this was because I've always been interested in engineering and, in fact, I originally had gone into the Air Force to be an engineer, not a pilot. Well, strangely enough, because the war had just ended in India and we were flying into China, I didn't want to go home in the least!
>
> The test pilots' school, which was then at Cranfield, started at the beginning of 1946. Because they were very short of test pilots, after half the course they took about twelve pilots and sent them to Boscombe Down to do performance testing and the rest of us were held in other jobs until the next course started. So, by the time we passed out it was the beginning of '47 and so I joined Farnborough in 1947. But I don't know why I was selected to be a test pilot.
>
> Don't forget, at that time we were very junior officers and knew very little, at least I knew very little about the RAF's development plans when I first went to Farnborough. All we had really was a succession of aeroplanes sent to us under development and all kinds of strange programmes. There was a tremendous lot going on in those days and an enormous number of aeroplanes.
>
> My first flight in a jet was in a Meteor 3. As soon as I got back from India, where I'd been flying DC-3s, I was about a week late for the start of the test pilots' school. It was the second day that I was there I think, they said, 'Oh, you've missed a week's lectures on these jets and how these jets work but you've got to fly one so off you go and fly one.' That was a most intriguing experience, although extremely simple to fly. The jet handling was, of course, extraordinary to anybody who hadn't done it before. The only instruction I really received on it was a hand my shoulder and, 'For goodness sake, watch your jet pipe temperatures which you must not go over.'

Whatever they were. And off we went. But, it was a strange, strange experience I must admit.

I suppose, not knowing anything at all about jet engines, I mean, to come back from flying in India and China, to come back to this totally strange power plant was eerie to say the least. But the great feature of the early jet engine was that you had to watch the jet pipe temperatures all the time because as soon as you went over the limits you ruined the engine and then there was this great surging problem that, strangely enough, when you first heard it you thought that the whole thing was coming to pieces but in fact it didn't seem to do any damage at all in those early centrifugal engines.

We flew Meteors and from time to time, Vampires. I suppose they were all much of a muchness. The Vampire was quite a nice little aeroplane to cut loose in and do some aerobatics in. But it was a docile little aeroplane.

Dickie Martin was made flight commander for the Aerodynamic Research Flight at the Royal Aircraft establishment at Farnborough. Here, he tested the early experimental jets that led to the development of the Hunter, Swift and Sea Vixen fighter aircraft, for which he was awarded the AFC in 1949:

It was exciting. We were particularly lucky at Farnborough because we had the most enlightened group captain and his policy was if you wanted to fly any aeroplane in any of the other flights, and the flight commander said it was alright, you had a go. There was no fussing about qualifications or whether a chap was fit to fly it or not. It was left to the people's common sense. In fact, I don't recall in the three years I was testing at Farnborough any occasion in which an aeroplane was broken.

I think we were all flying enthusiasts who enjoyed flying all these aeroplanes on these different experiments. We were a terribly light-hearted crowd and we enjoyed ourselves in the evenings and weekends to quite a large degree, and the thing about Farnborough was that the scientists who we were working for were also a lively crowd. So there was a wonderful mixture when you went out on a 'spree' in the evening, you were a mixture of boffins and RAF personnel. The design and

The Coronation Review of 1953. A watershed moment that enabled the Royal Air Force to showcase its might as it made the transition from piston power to jet power.

The Gloster E28/39 made its maiden flight at RAF Cranwell on 15 May 1941. It was powered by a single Frank Whittle designed Powerjets W.1 engine with a projected life of 10 hours. At the controls was Gloster's Chief Test Pilot Flight Lieutenant Gerry Sayer. (*BAE Systems*)

The Gloster Meteor F Mk1 was the first Allied jet which entered service with No 616 Squadron in July 1944. Aerodynamically conservative compared to the Me 262, it nevertheless brought the RAF and many air forces around the world into the jet age. (*BAE Systems*)

The de Havilland Vampire was the second jet to enter RAF service in 1946 and the first single engine jet fighter.

The shape of things to come. A prototype Avro Vulcan took part in the Coronation Review flypast although it did not enter service until 1956. (*BAE Systems*)

Jim Cooksey.

Jim Cooksey set the world record using a standard production Meteor F8.

John Cunningham by the DH108 'Swallow'

John Cunningham in front of a Mosquito night fighter.

de Havilland Vampire with a single Goblin turbojet at the SBAC show at Radlett.

The DH 110 'Sea Vixen' was the largest and most powerful of de Havilland's twin-boom fighters.

The first prototype of the DH 108 Swallow'. Chief Test Pilot Geoffrey de Havilland, son of the founder, is getting into the cockpit. Geoffrey de Havilland was killed in September 1946 while testing a DH 108. It is believed that the aircraft broke up while in a dive over the Thames Estuary.

JC in the cockpit of the DH 106 'Comet' the world's first jet airliner.

First Comet prototype G-ALVG in the air.

Above: DH Trident 1 G-ARPA BEA at Heathrow, August 1965.

Left: Eric Brown. The first FAA pilot to fly a jet, in December 1945, and the first person to land one – a de Havilland Vampire – on an aircraft carrier.

Grumman Martlet F-4F Mk.IV FN202 at Boscombe Down.

Deck landing a Sea Hornet. (*BAE Systems*)

Messerschmitt ME262 here seen in RAF markings as part of the Enemy Aircraft Flight.

Above left: Construction of the first Miles M52 was well advanced when the project was suddenly cancelled by the government.

Above right: DH100 Sea Vampire F1 landing on HMS *Ocean* 3 December 1945.

Above: English Electric Canberra B Mk1. (*BAE Systems*)

Left: Wing Commander Roland 'Bee' Beamont, CBE, DSO & Bar, DFC & Bar stepping from an English Electric Lightning T Mk4.

Lightning P1A (WG760) taking off at Warton during the Press Day 1955. (*BAE Systems*)

EE Lightning F6 with Beamont at the controls 1964. (*BAE Systems*)

BAC TSR2
(XR219) air
to air with its
problematic
undercarriage
deployed.
(*BAE Systems*)

Wing Commander
Richard 'Dickie'
Martin OBE
DFC & Bar AFC.

Air to air
photograph of
Gloster GA5
Javelin prototype
WD804.
(*BAE Systems*)

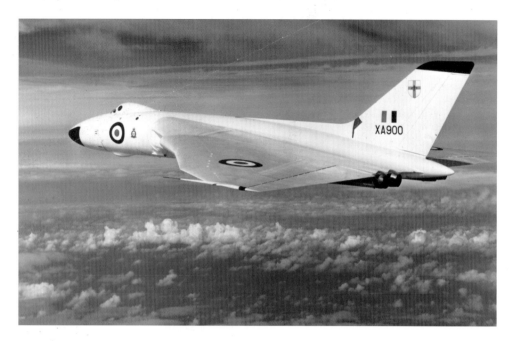

Above: Avro Vulcan B1 XA900 12th Mk 1. Instructional then scrapped 1986.

Left: Duncan Simpson OBE CEng FIMechE FRAeS.

Hawker Hunter prototype WB 188. (*BAE Systems*)

Above: Hawker
P1127 XP831 on
sortie from RAE
Bedford 1970.

Right: The first
Kestrel FGA1
in the colours
of the Tripartite
Evaluation
Squadron.
(*BAE Systems*)

Harrier GR1a
in the hover.
(*BAE Systems*)

Above: McDonnell
Douglas Harrier 2
of the United States
Marine Corps.

Left: Hawker Siddeley
Hawk prototype at
Farnborough 1974
(AFH Ltd).

Below left: Bristol 188
test pilot Godfrey Auty.

Below right: John 'Jo'
Lancaster.

Right: Bristol 188 two days before first flight in April 1962.

Below: Saunders-Roe SARO SR A-1 TG271 third prototype taking off in 1948.

Above left: The Armstrong Whitworth AW52. Jo Lancaster became the first British pilot to use an ejector seat when he experienced violent, uncontrollable vibration in an AW52.

Above right: John Allam Handley Page test pilot.

Handley Page HP80 better known as the Victor.

EE Lightning F.6 pair XS932 XR723 11 Squadron RAF refuel from Victor tanker c1969.

John Farley, with John Fozard – the Chief Designer of the Harrier – at Farnborough 1978 when the Sea Harrier FRS1 fighter variant for the RN was brand new.

The Short SC1.

Hawker P1127 in wooded scenario promo shot (*BAE Systems*).

Peter Twiss, Fairey test pilot.

Fairey Delta FD2 at Farnborough, 1956.

flying departments worked extremely closely together, not just on the job itself but socially.

Towards the end of my time in the Flight, which was around 1949 or '50, there was a great push to get the aeroplanes to go supersonic. Unfortunately, in the end, it was an American aeroplane which did just that.

I think the aerodynamicists and structural people at Farnborough were aware of the work done by German engineers during the war because right after the war there was a tremendous drive to go to places like Völkenrode and some of the other experimental places and find out what was happening and, indeed, several of the German scientists who were working there came to Farnborough, one of which was Doctor Karl Doetsch, who developed the first auto-stabiliser for the Meteor. He was working at Farnborough in those days.

We were very impressed with some of the designs that we found out about, which had, of course, not turned into aeroplanes. Even the ones that had – the Me 163 'Swallow' – which was never, in fact, flown under rocket power, I don't think, in England. But I think 'Winkle' Brown did some gliding tests with it and was quite impressed by its handling.

With the de Havilland 108, I think we were quite intrigued by the idea of flying an aeroplane without a tailplane and thinking that it might be the shape of aeroplanes to come. I wasn't greatly involved in the 108 programme. There were two versions at Farnborough: one we called the slow-speed one and a high-speed one. I did most of the flying on the slow-speed one, which was an investigation to see what the landing characteristics were like and what the low-speed handling was like. Unfortunately, it was met with disaster because after I had left the low-speed handling, a chap called (Squadron Leader George) 'Jumbo' Genders got killed in the slow-speed one. I took over Aero Flight before I left because a chap was killed in the high-speed one, (Squadron Leader Stuart) Muller-Roland, who was in charge of Aero Flight. It was quite a tricky aeroplane. It suffered from pitch oscillation at high speed, high up. If you got into an oscillation and held on to the control column you could aggravate it and we think that is probably what happened to Geoffrey de Havilland, who was killed in one over the Thames Estuary. The answer to pilot-induced oscillations was to let go of the stick but it obviously wasn't a feature you could accept in an aeroplane that was so sensitive.

With each mark of the early Meteors there was an increase in performance. The Mk 4 Meteor, as far as I remember, we did a programme on that because it had geared ailerons that were very sensitive to adjust. They were losing elevators, I think the elevator horns were breaking off. I seem to remember a programme on it.

I did three years testing at Farnborough, then I did a couple of years instructing test pilots and then the war college at Manby and then I did about eighteen months in the Air Ministry, which is how I wound up at Glosters. I was told that I was unlikely to get another flying job and I was sitting there as a wing commander in the Air Ministry just juggling paperwork thinking well this is not going to be the rest of my life and I resigned my Commission because I was offered this job at Glosters.

I think that it was a running down period for the Royal Air Force, everything was contracting really. In my day, which was 1951/52, it was a pretty dull life juggling paperwork at Richmond Terrace. The only consolation I had was that I was in charge of Handling Squadron, so I was able to get out every now and then and fly some of their aeroplanes.

After aircraft had been released by Boscombe Down, they were sent to the Handling Squadron and flown by ordinary squadron chaps to see what the Air Force was going to make of them and to write up the operating instructions for them, for the service, pilots' notes and so on.

I was responsible for all the publications concerned with flying training and I had a branch at the Ministry of Supply that did a lot of the paperwork for publishing and so on.

Following the election of the Labour government in July 1945, the new Prime Minister, Clement Attlee, declared that it was unlikely that Britain would face another major conflict in the foreseeable future. As a consequence, there would be no major defence spending for the next ten years. It was a decision that cost Britain's aircraft industry dearly. Having ended the war as world leaders in aviation development, Britain now began to fall behind.

The deepening of the Cold War reversed the position, although it would take several years to regain the ground already lost. The outbreak of the Korean War in 1950 and Britain's heavy involvement in the conflict only served to force the pace. A new specification was issued to Hawker and Supermarine for a new swept-wing fighter. Both companies put forward designs that would enter RAF service, the Hawker Hunter and the Supermarine Swift. The Swift was the first to fly in 1951, so becoming the RAF's first aircraft with swept wings and a swept tailplane:

> I only flew the Swift once I think, I don't know why I flew it, but it was a pretty brutal piece of machinery. It was certainly not a very appetising aeroplane, I think. Its wing loading was very high, but I only did one flight in it. I think I flew it at Chilbolton where the firm was based but all I remember is that it seemed to land at tremendous speed and I remember looking at the nipple on the end of the brake cable and thinking that if that comes off, it's going to be a very spectacular accident.

Although defence spending was reduced radically after the end of the Second World War, there was an acute awareness of the threat posed by jet bombers armed with nuclear weapons. For the time being, Britain's aerial defence would continue to rely on manned fighters as opposed to missiles. Although the RAF had plenty of day fighters like the Meteor and Vampire, there was a gap in its night-time capability. As a result, Gloster and de Havilland were given the go ahead for a new high-performance night fighter capable of intercepting a bomber at 40,000ft within eight minutes of engine ignition. Gloster's solution was the Javelin, which had a full delta wing and tailplane:

> I got to Glosters I think at the end of 1953 and I think the second (Javelin) prototype had been grounded after the (Commander Peter) Lawrence accident and the loss of the elevator on the first one. So I was flying Meteors for a couple of months, and so I think my first flight in the Javelin came probably in the spring of '54. It was the fourth Javelin and called E144, some funny designation in those days, WT830 I remember was its number.
>
> The Meteor had changed a lot. The Mk 8 was a good aeroplane. They'd got spring tab ailerons on it, which made it nice and manoeuvrable. Yes, it was a good aeroplane

It wasn't very difficult to move on to the Javelin. But, I don't remember it [first Javelin flight] at all, I think I've flow over 240 types and marks of aeroplane at Farnborough in my time and it was just another aeroplane, and, of course, it was very much restricted while they were sorting out the structural problems on the elevators and so on. As I remember, all the early flights I did in it were something quite harmless, like flying it round Malvern for the radar people to measure the radar profile or something like that.

I think the Javelin had three main problems. One was that the wings were too fat to make it go much above 0.9 Mach number. Second, we spent endless money and flights trying to stick vortex generators and things around the wing in order to get rid of the buffet at high Mach number. The stalling characteristics were pretty bad. The final thing, the one that made the project pretty useless, was of course, the radar. It was designed as an all-weather night fighter and to be successful at that, of course, you needed the latest in radar. We never got the collision course radar installed in it. Right up to the end we were still using virtually a wartime tail-chase radar, the AI17 and the AI22. So those were the three things that fixed the Javelin as a pretty unsuccessful aeroplane.

Not long after I took over the test flying, we were short of experimental pilots and so I borrowed a chap called Ross from Aero Flight in Farnborough. Tragically, he also got into a stall with it and went into the Severn Estuary and was killed. So, anyway, there was a long pause before we did anything more and then we fitted out an aeroplane with a tail parachute and guards over the tails and so on in order to do some further stalling tests. We then discovered that if you stalled, the thing automatically went into a spin, and a very erratic spin at that and a very unpredictable one. No two spins were ever the same. Some came out quite easily and other ones were jolly difficult to fish out. Finally, we thought we had got enough data on it to let Boscombe Down have a go but unfortunately as soon as the aeroplane got there they got it into a spin. Very unpredictable.

By the time it was operational it had stall warning devices on and, of course, the Air Force was forbidden to stall it and it had a stall warning on it.

Strangely, I don't think there was undue pressure put on us after the Javelin had been grounded [following fatal crashes]. The test pilots were important but they didn't play a defining role in the development. Funnily enough, the chap who always had the pressure put on him at Glosters was the chief stress man. I can remember him absolutely flatly refusing to allow an aeroplane to fly that was urgently wanted on a test because they hadn't completed the duplicate stressing on the aileron, I think it was the aileron or on the tail, something like that, and I can remember the chief designer going absolutely 'spare' trying to get this thing off the ground and the chief stress man saying, 'No, I'll not put my signature to it until I've done the calculations.' These men were of enormous integrity because they could really be pressurised. After all, a chap could take something out of the design office as a quick fix, manufacture it and unless the stress man could be convinced that it was safe, we didn't fly and that was great. I had every faith in the technical side.

We were a very close-knit team because, as far as Glosters was concerned, we had a separate Flight Development unit up at a place called Moreton Valence, which was about ten miles away from the main factory. So, we had our own aerodynamicist, our own little research department, inspection and so on, so it really was a very close-knit band of brothers.

I don't think we were overambitious. The one certain thing about the Air Force is, of course, all that training is exceptionally good. So, however awful the aeroplane is – or was – the training would cope with it because the flying trainers in the Air Force were exceptional, they could teach anybody to fly practically anything. They were very, very competent.

The Javelin entered service in 1956 with No. 46 Squadron and remained in service until 1968. By then Dickie Martin had moved on in 1960 to become a test pilot at A.V. Roe, where he soon found himself flying another delta-winged aircraft, the Vulcan:

I'm a lucky chap to have flown a lot of aeroplanes. But my favourite aeroplane? I think my favourite one of all was the Vulcan. That really was a fun aeroplane. Another one I really

93

did enjoy, at one stage in my Flight I had a B-17, a Flying Fortress. That was a super aeroplane, it really was. Like a huge, great Anson, absolutely viceless.

I'd flown a lot of big, four-engine aeroplanes in my day, in fact before I went up to Avros I'd done almost a year on the Argosy at Bitteswell. But nothing I had flown was much of a help as far as the Vulcan was concerned. That was really quite a different aeroplane altogether. Because it didn't have flaps, it only had air brakes. If you weren't used to them, your first attempts to land it ended up in colossal overshoots because you couldn't get the speed off and if you came in a little fast it was very, very slippery and everything sailed past and you missed it altogether. So you had to be aware of the technique of getting the speed right and getting the attitude up a bit in order to land it. You could pick up quite large amounts of yaw if you weren't concentrating. After about five or six hours, of course, you never thought about it, it was second nature. But the early flights were quite interesting! I remember doing my first flights with Jimmy Harrison and he was laughing his head off as I made my first two attempts to get into Woodford.

We were privileged, of course, because we could fly it at weights that the Service would probably never fly it at. In other words, on a retest you could put in 25,000lb of fuel, which is ridiculously low, and then, of course, it went off the ground at about 18,000ft a minute practically vertically. It was a terrific roller coaster of an aeroplane in flight. You could really zoom about in it. It handled very nicely. It was very easy to forget sitting up at the front of it that there was a big aeroplane hanging out of the back.

I reckon, if light, it would have out-climbed a Javelin. The other salient thing about it was the engine handling on the Bristol Olympus, amazing! You could put the throttle from idle, straight up to the stops and the engine would accelerate to full power in six seconds, which was phenomenal whereas the Javelin, the early Javelins, in fact we used to do it on production test to make sure it met the specification, I think we passed them out in those days if they went not more than seventeen seconds from idle to full power. That's a hell of a time – seventeen seconds from idle to full power.

I don't think that caused any operational problems, except that you obviously had to be very careful not to make an approach with a very low throttle right back because you were high and then have to overshoot because you had to remember it was going to take you seventeen seconds to get your power back on again.

Looking back, the early jets were fairly simple. It's very difficult over a distance of fifty years to differentiate between these aeroplanes. I think I flew over 240 marks of aeroplane so, that's a lot of aeroplanes, and it's very difficult to keep clear in your mind at great distance what their differences were. I mean, you only got to fly something like the Spearfish once and it's seared into your mind forever after. That's for sure! Appalling! The poor old Navy really did have some pretty desperate aeroplanes, although the Spearfish never did make it into service, thank God!

Although the DH.110 was a good one and the Buccaneer was good (although I never got to fly one). But those early ones were terrible: the Skuas, 'bogging' around in Swordfish and Fulmars, dreadful, dreadful stuff! I managed to get a flight in a DH.110. I thought it was a very good aeroplane. I have a feeling I was briefed on it by John Derry at Hatfield and I remember asking him what were the limitations and I think he said it was something like 605 knots and 5½G and I said, Well what about other Mach numbers,' as we were absolutely loaded with restrictions on the Javelin, and he said there weren't any, you could go as fast as you like. I thought, 'My gosh, this is quite an aeroplane,' and it handled very nicely. I think it was originally a 'banker' specification for the RAF if the delta-wing project turned out impossible.

The other thing about the 110 was, of course, it had this collision warning radar in it so it was a good aeroplane, except I wouldn't have liked to have been the radar operator, who was in a pretty difficult position down on one side, so his escape prospects were not very good.

We used to try and drum this into the students on the test pilots' school. All you're really required to do is to carry out the programme provided you consider it safe. Do that very accurately – and this is the old days, of course now it's all recorded – and say what happened, not what you think happened or ought to happen but what actually has happened. That is much harder than you would imagine, so the chap that could do that was the person the technical people really wanted because you, the test pilot, couldn't solve the aerodynamics of the thing or the engineering but as long as you told them exactly what you had done and what had happened then there was hope. But, nowadays, of course, the whole lot is recorded or telemetered down and so they can see very quickly by how much your air speed deviates on the climb.

While he was at Glosters, Dickie Martin encouraged a group of apprentices to broaden their knowledge by helping rebuild a Gloster Gladiator – a fighter that had been in service before the Second World War. Dickie Martin had begun flying aircraft in the Shuttleworth Collection in 1948 and it was with great pride that he and the team of apprentices were able to present the Trust with their Gladiator restored to flying condition. He continued to fly the Shuttleworth's vintage aircraft for many years and remained on the executive committee for forty-two years. He died on 1 September 2006.

Duncan Simpson

Duncan Simpson was born on 23 December 1927 in Edinburgh. From an early age he knew he wanted to fly:

> I wanted to become a test pilot because I had an uncle who was chief test pilot for the Fairey Aviation company during the First World War and I was always interested in flying. I had the idea that I would like to be involved one day from a very early age, long before school days, and I think I was fired up by going to Alan Cobham's Flying Circus in 1934 in the north of Scotland and that really got me going.
>
> I tried to join the RAF at the end of the war, but they didn't really think much of people going in to train as pilots at that time, so I decided to go to the de Havilland company and spent four years learning something about aeroplanes. It was a marvellous time to do it because of all the exciting projects in the de Havilland company.
>
> I was just doing my student's apprenticeship with the De Havilland company through the technical school. But, of course, after we had done one year of basic training we were sent out into the shops at Hatfield and I was lucky enough to be assigned to the experimental shops, where there was some pretty exciting things happening.
>
> I think it's fair to say de Havillands were right at the forefront. They had the DH.106 Comet airliner, which was quite a long way ahead of anybody else and the fact that they had problems later on was a real tragedy because we were leading the world at that time in that particular sphere. And, of course, the light transport, the Dove, was incredibly successful quite apart from their military aeroplanes. Out of the war came

the Mosquito and the Hornet, the Vampire – one of the first jet aeroplanes – a single engine as opposed to the Meteor, which was a twin-engine aeroplane, and later the Venom, which was just in its infancy when I was still working there.

I think the British aircraft industry was still in its wartime rundown state, although it was an incredibly capable industry right across the board: aircraft, engines, airframes military and civil and a lot of prototypes were emerging from the various well-known companies like de Havillands and Hawkers and Gloster.

I joined the Air Force as I said I would in 1949 and went through the initial jet training in its very early days when they were training quite a number of RAF pilots on the early versions of the Meteor. I then joined an operational Meteor squadron, where I spent two and a half years flying one of my favourite aeroplanes, which was the Meteor Mk 8, on No. 222 Squadron in Fighter Command.

I was trained to fly on Harvards and I think it's fair to say that if you could be reasonably competent in the Harvard you could fly almost anything that the service asked you to fly. It was a magnificent trainer. Then it was straight onto the Meteor T.7, the two-seat version, followed by solo flying on the Meteor Mk 4 at the operational conversion unit before you went to the squadron.

The Meteor T.7 and Mk 4 were very similar in terms of the layout of the aeroplane. It wasn't until the Mk 8 came in that you had the ejector seat fitted and a much-improved tail unit and flying controls. which made the handling of the aeroplane much better. The Meteor Mk 8 was a great favourite. It was a beautiful aeroplane to fly, very forgiving and had two marvellous Rolls-Royce Derwent engines, which believe me, flying over Scotland at night in winter was a great comfort as opposed to the single-engine contemporaries.

The asymmetric flying problem on the Meteor could be as large as you wanted to make it. The training system in the Air Force was very, very severe indeed to teach you how to cope with asymmetric emergencies and I often felt they went much too far in teaching people to fly under extreme emergency on one engine at an altitude that gave you very little time for recovery if things went wrong. There were a lot of accidents, no doubt about it, and I spoke to Roly Beamont about this and he was very much for saying that the Canberra was the same. We could have done this in a slightly safer way. But it certainly prepared you for anything that was going to come your way later on but by and large if you did have an engine failure, maybe not on take-off but later in the flight, flying on one engine in these aeroplanes was very straightforward and the recovery was also very straightforward unless you found an obstruction on the runway and had to overshoot on one, then you had to be quite careful about what you were about.

Of course, having been trained at the de Havillands, I wanted to go and fly Vampires. In fact, there weren't any vacancies at the time so I went on to Meteors. I flew them both – I flew the Vampires with the auxiliary squadrons at weekends. That was quite exciting. But the Vampire was a small aeroplane. It didn't have the performance of the Meteor and it didn't have the load carrying but it was a very agile little aeroplane. It manoeuvred extremely well and was a great favourite. But one mustn't forget that the Vampire was developed quite drastically by putting the de Havilland Ghost engine in, which had another 2,000lb of thrust, and a new wing – a thin wing – which was called the Venom. That was quite an aeroplane. It was a performer, a very effective little aeroplane both at high altitude and low altitude. In fact, it was the only thing that would go to substantially over 50,000ft in Fighter Command at that time.

We used to take part in the annual summer exercise, where we would literally be invaded from Europe with various European air forces and the American Air Force. It really was quite realistic in that with bad weather and all the things you have to contend with, it was quite like the real thing.

The North American B-45 Tornado, I remember, was one of the favourite targets on exercises, and the Canberras. They used to act as targets coming in for Fighter Command to intercept in those days. Fighter Command had a very large number of aeroplanes and squadrons at that time, Meteors mainly and Vampires.

After my squadron tour when I went on to the Fighter Development Unit we were flying about six or seven different types of new fighter including the F-86 from the States – the Sabre – and the new British transonic fighters, the Supermarine Swift and the Hunter. It was very interesting to see how they stacked up against the opposition coming in.

The Swift was rather more than slightly disappointing! When I went to the development squadron, we were flying the F-86 and the Venom. The Venom was mainly doing high flying trials with specially prepared Venoms. They were unpainted, anything to save weight, one radio set and we wore pressure breathing waistcoats and pressure masks to go up into the region of 53–54,000ft, being the only aeroplane that could operate at those heights.

The Sabre we were using as a comparison between the typical American-type fighter and our own British ones. We were looking forward to receiving our first transonic British aeroplane, the Swift Mk 1, in January '54. I'm afraid the Swift Mk 1 was a big disappointment, and I must stress this, as an interceptor fighter. Later on, they developed it as a very successful PR [photo reconnaissance] and FR [fighter reconnaissance] type at low level in Germany. But it wasn't until they got the Hunter in July 1954 that we got an aeroplane that had the promise of being the equal of the American aeroplanes. The Hunter Mk 1 arrived in July and the Hunter Mk 2 followed it closely with the Sapphire engine. It was shortly after that that I joined the Hawker Aircraft company. The Hunter, I'm afraid, led me astray!

I didn't begin test flying until 1954, when I took part in the test flying of several new fighters at the Central Fighter Establishment at West Raynham when I was in the RAF and that was really the beginning of it. From there I joined Hawker Aircraft when the Hunter was just starting production and remained with them for twenty-four years.

I was always very conscious of the danger because, of course, it was inherent in the flying business, particularly in military flying. In those days we did have a lot of accidents. But I think one was so focused on wanting to do it that one sort of took it in one's stride.

The F-86 was the first operational aeroplane to exceed the speed of sound. In saying that, you could only achieve the speed of sound by pointing it vertically downwards, you couldn't do it in any other sort of regime of flight. It was fast, it handled extremely well – beautiful flying controls, it was comfortable – lovely cockpit, everything that the pilot wanted. Its only drawback, as far as we were concerned, as an interceptor was that it was very slow in getting off the ground. The engine start on the J-47 engine was very slow and the time to height was not always good. But for what the Americans were using it for in Korea up over the Yalu River it could take its time to get up there and, of course, when it was up there and into combat it dropped its tanks and it was extremely effective against the Chinese opposition but a very different aeroplane from our own Venom. To give you a comparison, we did our scramble take-off with four Venoms for a visiting American team. We had four Venoms off the ground in forty-eight seconds. Well, it took over forty seconds to start the engine on the Sabre and the Americans were very impressed with that. The Venom was a very effective little aeroplane, very manoeuvrable.

Just as I had left the Air Force, my contemporaries at the Fighter Establishment went across to fly the F-100 Super Sabre but I was safely at Hawkers at that time and I missed it. But the Sabre went into squadron service in some numbers, particularly in Germany. That was the Mk 4 Sabre, as we called it in the Air Force, the F-86E, which we had at West Raynham. We did also fly the later ones with the Canadair Orenda engine, which was a much, much better aeroplane because it had a lot more performance, a lot more thrust, and in fact the Sabre Mk 6 with the Orenda was the direct competitor with the Hunter Mk 9 for the Swiss contract, which we won with the Hunter. But very similar performance.

I think the Hunter won the contract because both these aircraft had to satisfy all the Swiss mountain requirements in terms of pure performance and operations in the Swiss mountains. I think the Hunter won it on its armament. We had four very big 30mm Aden guns and the Swiss were very impressed with the Hunter's armament.

The early Hunters suffered with problems when firing the Aden cannon. Exhaust gases were sucked into the engine causing surging and flame outs at altitude. Also, the spent links from the ammunition belts tumbled along the fuselage causing much damage:

> I think Rolls-Royce used to say it was the Hawker intakes and Hawkers used to say it was the engine problems. It was a mixture of all sorts of things. They had to get the surge margins right so that you didn't suffer from gun gases going into the front of the engine and making it surge. It was a very complex problem. Rolls-Royce are very good on these things since it's a big organisation and once Rolls-Royce gets the bit between their teeth they will solve these problems and they went to town on this, on the Avon engine, and eventually we got what we wanted. With the gun firing while manoeuvring at high angles of incidence and large angles of sideslip, you know, in combat manoeuvres, in the early aeroplanes the engine would surge and, of course, if it surged to such a degree that it went out you had to relight it and that was not very good news. It had to be fixed.

A solution to the problems was found by mounting the cannon in blisters on the underside of the fuselage but there were many other faults that hindered the Hunter's development:

> The Hunter started off in Mk 1 and Mk 2 form with two different engines. There were a lot of very basic faults: cabin air conditioning, demisting, de-icing on the cockpit, engine surging on the engine. Once we had developed it for two or three years with the Air Force and Boscombe Down taking part, the big Avon engine was put in it and that transformed the aeroplane. All the other shortcomings were put-rightable. Very simply, it was just a matter of time and money but in Mk 9 form it was probably one of the best-engineered airframe combinations, which stood up to anything the pilots would give it. He could slam the engine around, he could fire his guns up to 50,000ft, it was a very highly developed aeroplane. We sold it to twenty countries overseas and it was in service with twenty-two air forces. If we had had more time and more airframes, we could have sold a lot more of them but we were devoting our energies to rather more important matters in the early '60s.

I think the two different engines were put in as an insurance policy. They were two different engines in terms of handling and the performance. The Sapphire was in fact, the most promising engine in terms of handling but it was not as reliable as the Avon. Eventually they got the two characteristics brought together in the big Avon engine. They also developed a big Sapphire which I think, only did six flights in the Hunter and it was not continued with. The Avon continued as the 203 Avon engine and proved such a successful engine that we persevered with it right through the Hunter history to many overseas customers.

The Hawker Hunter remains one of the all-time great fighter aircraft, seeing service in twenty-one overseas air forces as well as the RAF. In fact, in 2014, sixty years after its original introduction, Hunters were still in service with the Lebanese Air Force. But Duncan Simpson's career was to take a new direction when he became test pilot on what was to become the Harrier:

I was exposed to the P.1127, not in the first instance because only two pilots, Bill Bedford and Hugh Merewether, were involved to start off with. I flew it in 1962 and was gradually absorbed into the programme, first of all on the prototypes and then on the trials aeroplane, the Kestrel, which took part in the American–German–British trials for this new concept, not just a new aeroplane. But, being a test pilot at Hawkers, I was more or less brought in as the No. 3 pilot when requirements arose.

I had been watching its progress very closely at Dunsfold for the two years before I flew it. In fact, I was probably one of the most experienced watchers of any aircraft programme. It was quite an exciting time to be around, I don't mind admitting, and although we did not have many serious incidents with it in the prototype and Kestrel years, most of the problems started when we were getting it into service with extending the engine and airframe. We had quite a few problems in the late '60s and early '70s, which I think we would have rather done without, but eventually it has become a very, very reliable bit of kit. When you look at the subsequent history in the Falklands and later the operational squadrons using the Mk 7 it is very rewarding to see how this came about over the years.

I remember my first Harrier flight fairly clearly because I was used as a guinea pig in that I was subjected to as little helicopter flying as I possibly could. In fact, I only did three thirty-five-minute trips in a helicopter at the Empire Test Pilots' school. Then I got straight into the P.1127 prototype. One had to concentrate extremely hard in those days on exactly what you were doing because it was all new. I just had to take what I was told as being the thing to do. Concentrate and do what I was told, and it was quite straightforward. In fact, if I had thought that the P.1127 prototype was as difficult as the S-51 helicopter at the Empire Test Pilots' school I think I would have been put off it for good because that helicopter was not my idea of fun. But the P.1127, provided you did what was briefed, it was very straightforward and a little bit of an anticlimax in a way.

It was a completely new dimension, to be able to take the nozzle lever, pull it back and gradually increase thrust until the aircraft was fully supported on the engine. Of course, one of the most difficult aspects of the aeroplane was the flying controls, which had to work at all speeds from 600mph right down to the hover, even flying backwards, sideways and manoeuvring. That was a tremendous technical achievement by the design team at Hawkers. We had a lot of very clever people working on this project and it was quite an eye-opener to fly it, a privilege.

The men behind the Harrier were very single-minded people. Sir Sydney Camm and Sir Stanley Hooker were great personalities. They had extremely strong design teams on both the engine and the airframe, and Ralph Hooper and John Fozard, who were the leading designers on the P.1127 and Harrier project, were backed up by a very strong team. But Sir Sydney Camm and Sir Stanley Hooker got on very well together, which was a great thing in the project's favour, to have two very powerful people at the top of the design teams, and they saw to it that no interference from outside quarters would be tolerated. In fact, it was so good that the P.1127 prototype was built and flown in only eighteen months, which was a real triumph of manufacture and experimental engineering.

Today's multinational programmes take a lot longer because they've all got their own requirements, they've all got their own specifications. Fortunately, we were on our own at Hawkers and we could pretty well make changes over night. In fact, it was not only like that on the Harrier, it was the same on the Hawk. We had to work very, very quickly to get those aeroplanes into service on cost and on time.

The Kestrel was a development out of the P.1127 prototypes, of which there were six built and the sixth prototype was really the aeroplane built to the same specification as the trials aircraft, which was called the Kestrel. We built nine of them, which the German air force, the RAF, the American army, navy and air force flew as an international squadron to look at the sort of operational capabilities of this sort of aeroplane. The irony of course, was that it was the United States Marine Corps who bought the aeroplane. They came in in 1968 about four years after the tripartite trials and when they saw it they said, 'We're going have it' and that I think was the spur we needed to really get the Harrier into service jointly with what the Americans called the AV-8A, which was the American version.

The big problem was to get it into RAF service with minimum trouble, certainly without anything that could be levelled at the aeroplane's principles of flight so that the disbelievers couldn't snipe at it. It was a very important time in that the Air |Force selected four instructors who were very experienced ground-attack people to form the nucleus of the operational conversion unit. But before the unit was started these four pilots were sent down to our airfield at Dunsfold and I was more or less detailed to instruct them in the basic flying of the Harrier. Once they'd done that, which they had done within five hours flying, once they were checked out on the aeroplane, we flew the aeroplanes up to RAF Wittering. That was the start of the RAF training programme because all that ten years of development would have been worth nothing if we didn't get the aeroplane into service. That is the test, to get it operating in the service and, of course, we were looking forward to seeing it operating in the United States Marine Corps as well. But all the training was done at Wittering by the Royal Air Force.

To begin with, pilots had to do their training on the single-seat fighters. This was far from ideal in such a complex aircraft that offered so many new capabilities. A two-seat version was ordered in 1967 to assist pilots in the conversion process. The prototype T.2 first flew in 1969 and it was while test flying a T.2 that Duncan Simpson had to eject at 3,000ft after experiencing engine failure. Despite breaking his neck, he was back testing nine months later. By then, the United States Marine Corps were showing a keen interest, although a potential stumbling point was that the Harrier was a British aircraft while the US armed forces always had a preference for 'buy American':

> Working with the Americans really wasn't an issue in that we had such a close relationship with first of all, the United States Marine Corps, then we went into partnership with McDonnell Douglas. We had a lot of our design staff go over there, work with them and, of course, it resulted in a very successful partnership in developing the AV-8A into the AV-8B, which was the aeroplane that the Marine Corps really wanted in terms of their requirements and, of course, it ended up with the Royal Air Force buying the aeroplane that eventually became the GR5 and GR7. But the Navy aeroplane came about in a slightly different way. But it was a very happy partnership with the Americans and very beneficial to both.

The partnership with the Americans arguably saved the Harrier as there were many who felt that it was too much of an innovation with limited utility:

> The Germans decided to go their own way with the VAK 191, which became too complicated and really too difficult to get into production and they never really got very far with it. The French likewise did not proceed beyond the prototype stage for the Mirage 3V and the Americans really went to the Brits to get themselves an aeroplane for the Marine Corps.
>
> There were people around in the late '60s after all the cancellations and the '70s who really felt that this was too much of an innovation for military aviation. They wanted supersonics, they wanted all sorts of things. We tried to persuade them that this aeroplane would do something and operate in a way that no other aeroplane could operate in. Of course, it was proved in the Falklands. If we hadn't had the

Harrier we wouldn't have done anything and there it was doing everything that Hawkers and the believers in the Ministry of Defence said it would. But we had a lot of opposition politically and from inside the service. But gradually people began to realise that with the new weapons coming in, the platform did not have to be supersonic. It had a higher subsonic capability and manoeuvrability where it could look after itself against its contemporaries and I will say that from the Falklands war, an aeroplane that is supersonic, that's operating at the end of its range when it's got external stores on it, and is forced to fly subsonic, it's very much worse off than the subsonic aeroplane that is designed specifically for the purpose and the Harrier shot them out of the sky. No doubt about it.

I think the US Marines thought they had discovered something when they put the nozzles down and found this was an extremely effective air brake. This was quite true, and we didn't know about this. But where we were in trouble was that when you put the nozzles down at high speeds, it produced very high loads in the nozzle system and interconnecting chains and links, and we were very concerned that it would lead to structural failure. We told them to steady on, because we were looking at this. We were going to strengthen up the whole system in the engine to put up with very high loads. Once we'd done that we could investigate what they called the vectoring thrust in forward flight because, no doubt about it, it was the best air brake you'd got. There was a misconception that it would add to the manoeuvrability if you put the nozzles down. If you work it out, it didn't. What it did do was provide a very effective air brake. Anything following you, if you put your nozzles down at high speed, would simply overshoot and you could make their life very difficult. Then, of course, you could immediately pop the nozzles back up again and re-accelerate and chase whatever you were chasing. Very effective but totally unexpected and by chance. I forget what they cleared it up to. I think it was something like 400 knots plus, but, of course, the aeroplane was quite a draggy aeroplane, so if you throttled back it decelerated. But, of course, you had got an air brake as well but it was just an additional method of shaking off the enemy, so to speak.

I stopped flying Harriers in the mid-'70s. The Mk 5 was really a different aeroplane. Basically, the flying controls and the engine were very similar but the avionics and electronics and the improved handling, I'm told, improved it tremendously. But I can only say what my successors told me. I believe it was a very pleasant aeroplane to fly, a very much easier plane to fly in many ways because of the auto stabilisation. We would have loved to have had that but it was far too heavy to have in the early days so we didn't have it but they were able to develop this magic kit.

Towards the end of the 1960s it was quite obvious that the Royal Air Force would need a new advanced trainer. The Gnat was coming to the end of its useful life and there were certainly aspects of the Gnat which weren't very suitable for advanced training for the big aeroplanes. It did a wonderful job for the time that it was in service, particularly with the Red Arrows, but an advanced trainer was obviously going to be necessary. At Hawkers we were very keen to be involved in this new trainer. We had the expertise from the Hunter and, of course, from the Harrier and the design team, the manufacturing team, and the development team were all in place and we won whatever competition there was to produce the RAF's new trainer. We had an excellent relationship between our design staff and the Royal Air Force trainers, the instructors.

The Hawker P.1182 was the type number that eventually came about and it was named the Hawk. The prototype aeroplane was built at Kingston and it flew for the first time at Dunsfold on 21 August 1974. It was an aeroplane that was designed very carefully to have a big cockpit because I think we all realised that the Hawk T1 for the Royal Air Force was just the beginning. We had to develop it, we had to put a lot more operational equipment in it and sell it overseas. Eventually, in addition to the T1s for the Air Force that were going through, which were fairly basic advanced trainers, we built our own demonstrator in which we installed weapon-aiming facilities, weapons carriage, to offer to overseas air forces in the hope that it would be as successful as the Hunter, which sold so well overseas. In fact, looking back all these years on the Hawk development and the sales, it has been incredibly successful and was still going strong in the year 2001, although I must confess, I left it behind some twenty-five years ago.

With the project pilots Andy Jones and Jim Hawkins, I was lucky enough to have two up-to-date project pilots from the Air Force. We were involved with the project right from the drawing board and I think I can say that we all flew it within the first five flights and I think all three of us were very impressed with what Hawkers had produced. It was very comfortable, smooth, it had a good turn of performance, good endurance, very good vision from both front and rear cockpits. With the rear cockpit where the instructor was going to sit for the next forty or fifty years it was terribly important to give him a good environment, good vision out of the rear cockpit. We developed a hood arc to quite a high standard. It's been a very successful little aeroplane and then, of course, the Red Arrows have shown it off literally, all over the world. They've done tours to America, South Africa, out into the Pacific and the reliability is quite outstanding.

Comparing the Hawk with the Vampire and Meteor and advanced trainers in the late '40s and '50s, in many ways the Hawk, being a subsonic aeroplane, we go back to the same sort of aerodynamics, in a way, although the Hawk is transonic. You can dive it as fast as you like but we had to make several changes to the wing to enable us to do this. We had to get the stalling and the spinning sorted out so that it could be fully cleared for the Royal Air Force. The time to develop the handling to the standard required through Boscombe Down to the Air Force was about two years three months, which is about as quickly as you could have possibly done it. But we spent a lot of time in getting the low-speed and medium-speed, and indeed the high-speed, handling to the required standard. It worked out very well.

In fact, the Americans were more than interested. The United States Navy involved the Hawk in their advanced trainer competition, which in fact, it won, and it went into the United States Navy as part of a training package known as the T-45. The Americans modified it fairly extensively but not radically in order to do carrier landings. They 'beefed up' the undercarriage and put a hook on it and did all the good things that naval aircraft have on them but it was a very big contract. We again worked with McDonnell Douglas, which we'd worked with on the Harrier in the United States, so that was a very big breakthrough to let the Americans buy the Hawk.

The Hawk will go on for a long time because what they are doing now is putting the same instruments as the modern fighters into the Hawk cockpit. This could go on for years because you're still training the same type of pilot, the task has not changed really; you're still training the same type of individual human being on a very much more advanced aeroplane. But you don't need a very much more advanced aeroplane in the way of performance. The Hawk has got quite good enough performance to introduce the pilot in to military flying to enable him to go on to the F-16, F-18-type aeroplanes, and indeed the Eurofighter.

I think we [the British aviation industry] probably did lose out a bit. In the UK, when we were dealing with our own Hawker aeroplanes, we were very much our own masters. We didn't have to refer to European collaborators and, of course, we could cut the corners. But these projects now are so big that you just can't do it as a national project, so you have to team up with other partners. But it is a very much longer gestation period.

I suppose you could say we were always the final arbiter in getting the aeroplane right because if we missed things or if we made mistakes, they would only reappear when they went up to the Air Force for service testing. So there was no point in shelving faults until later on. We were always very keen at Hawkers on getting service test pilots in at a very early stage on the flight development. If you had got a two-seater aeroplane you could not only get them in on the problem but you could fly with them and say look, what do you think of this? That way, it gave us much more power to our elbow to get the problem sorted out. At the Hawker company we were always very lucky in that the chief test pilot and his pilots were never put under pressure by the company. We always had the direct line to the chief designer, and the general manager for that matter, and the chairman. He used to come down to Dunsfold and talk with us, and if we were particularly concerned about anything they would listen very carefully and eventually we would get it put right long before it went too far. We were very lucky.

What makes a good test pilot? I think the first thing you've got to prove is that you can fly an aeroplane and probably fly it to an above-average standard. Then, I think it's a great advantage to have an engineering or technical training and I think nowadays you can't enter the business without going through the Empire Test Pilots' School, that is a must, and probably follow that with a tour of test flying in the Royal Air Force or the Royal Navy, no doubt about that. It has all got so complicated and you need so much more technical training that that is a must. There are very, very few slots for people flying the front-line prototype aeroplanes, very few indeed.

I don't think not flying during the war was a disadvantage. In fact, I was very relieved not to be a wartime pilot in a way because I probably wouldn't have survived. But a lot of those people brought operational experience, which you couldn't get any other way. We worked with them so much. On my squadron half the pilots were ex-wartime people. On the Fighter Development Unit, probably three-quarters of them had wartime experience. I was on a short service commission and never had that experience, but we were working together and flying together, and I learnt a lot from them in a big way.

We didn't have the Javelin at the Fighter Development Unit, at least, not in my time. At Hawkers, which was part of the Hawker Siddeley Group, we often used to go across and fly each other's aeroplanes and at one stage when things were a little bit slack at Dunsfold I was asked to go across and help the Gloster test pilots with some test flying on the Javelin. This was at the time that the Javelin was pretty fully developed in the Mk 8 and the Mk 9. But I was fascinated because the Javelin was very much a developed and upgraded Meteor. It was a typical Gloster aeroplane. It was big and strong and very effective. Whatever criticisms anybody had of a Javelin, it was a very effective means, as an all-weather fighter, of getting guided weapons up through 40,000ft of cloud and back down again as an all-weather fighter with two crew and guided weapons. It was an effective aeroplane; much bigger than the fighters I had flown but I was very interested to fly it.

I think you could tell which manufacturer made a particular aeroplane. I think the Hawker cockpit was very much a Hawker cockpit and a de Havilland cockpit was a de Havilland cockpit. They all had their idiosyncrasies and you could pretty well tell where they came from. A Hawker cockpit was fairly roomy because all the test pilots seem to be very big chaps and we didn't like being restricted in our getting in and out of aeroplanes. The Venom cockpit with an ejector seat in, I was only just eligible to fly the Venom because my knees would foul the windscreen on ejection with the ejector seat, but some of the military aeroplanes and the manufacturers and the Air Force didn't stand too much on comfort as far as cockpits were concerned. Some of them were incredibly uncomfortable until later on when we paid a lot of attention to the comfort of the seats and the comfort of the cockpit, the ergonomics of the thing, and they became much better. Sometimes you have to spend quite a long time in these aeroplanes. The Harriers going out to the South Atlantic were flying for nine hours with flight refuelling. To be cooped up in a single-seat cockpit for nine hours is almost beyond my understanding but that's the sort of operations they were involved in.

It became very competitive in the '70s when overseas air forces, by and large, had their own evaluation teams. They had to come over and fly in our aircraft, and hardly a week went by without our test pilots being involved in sales activities. Of course, it was a tremendous advantage to have been involved in the development of the aeroplane to talk to overseas potential customers and then, of course, if they did buy the aeroplane, to follow up the sale by going and training the overseas air forces to fly. With the Hunter, of course, we went all over the world. We were very lucky in places like South America, Asia, Switzerland, Sweden, the Benelux countries. We saw a lot of very interesting flying taking place in overseas air forces. They didn't all operate the aeroplane in the same way. They all had their own requirements and characteristics, and some of it was quite exciting, in South America among the Andes and in Switzerland amongst the Alps. We had plenty of that sort of work. Some people liked that more than others. Some people were very dedicated to the flight development side of a business, but we had to – and some people were very good at it – go overseas and mix with foreign air forces and deliver aeroplanes.

I think it [the British aircraft industry] lost a lot of its charisma but I think the way it has gone is the only way it could have gone. The first big change I saw just before I stopped test flying was the joining up of Hawker Siddeley and the British Aircraft Corporation. I think everybody realised that it was going to be inevitable that these two were going to merge to form what was eventually called British Aerospace and that it had to work and everybody in those two companies right from the top to the bottom had to make certain that it did work, and it did, very successfully.

I think when we look back on it [late '40s/50s] we were very, very conscious of the fact that we were privileged to fly a lot of aeroplanes in the industry under development that were the result of years of work by the technical department, not only the design team, but on the manufacturing side of it and the experimental shops where people had worked night and day on bringing these aeroplanes together, some very skilled work which I saw very largely in my own apprenticeship when I was working in the experimental shop at Hatfield. But I admired the people that did it tremendously. At the end of the day, when it came to be flown, it was a big responsibility to fly these prototype aeroplanes on which so much depended and in which so much work was invested and money, of course. Prototype aeroplanes cost a great deal of money and it wasn't just the future of the aeroplane, it was the future of the company at stake, at Hawkers, where we were concentrating on fighter aeroplanes, and at de Havillands, where they had an even bigger spread of civil and military projects. But, of course, the jet V/STOL business was a widespread task in itself, which was a great privilege to take part in, even in a small way.

In 1978 Duncan Simpson retired from test flying. But he still 'kept his hand in' through his involvement with the Historic Aircraft Association, of which he was a founder member. He continued to fly and preserve historic aircraft including the Lysander, Sea Fury and a Hurricane. He died on 5 December 2017.

Godfrey Auty

Born in 1921, Godfrey Auty enjoyed a test flying career that spanned the first generation of jets including the Meteor and Vampire through to experimental aircraft that helped create Concorde:

> I originally wanted to fly because of the war as I was the right sort of age. I used to see these sorts of sporting club-type aeroplanes flying around from time to time and it always fascinated me and when the war started I volunteered as a pilot and that's how it all began really.
>
> The Hampden was an unusual-shaped aeroplane, but I liked the aeroplane very much. It was a very stable aeroplane and it had this narrow fuselage so one had a very good forward view and also the canopy, you could slide back. We were flying at the time between Vancouver Island and Vancouver doing torpedo dropping with it. It was the ideal aeroplane for that and I thoroughly enjoyed that. It was a great opportunity to fly something unusual.
>
> Well I think it did stand me in good stead. I think I was very fortunate because I got the opportunity to fly a lot of aeroplanes, I got a wide experience of aircraft handling and so forth, and it was all very interesting. I enjoyed it.
>
> I think a good test pilot has got to understand the workings of the aeroplane, know the systems and so forth and the engine and know a lot about it from the technical side. Now, with the fast aeroplanes one needs to know more about the aerodynamic side of it as well. Apart from reading books, there wasn't always a great deal of information for the high-speed flying but generally speaking I think it's something that has built up over the time. After the war I was test flying Spitfires

and Tempests and the other fast aeroplanes, and then the jet aircraft, which started with a conversion from piston to jet, a Vampire, and then flying Meteors and Venoms. Again, having flown a lot of different aircraft in the Royal Air Force, I then joined the Bristol Aeroplane Company in 1951 and we were flying Meteors there for a short time, which were on overhaul and one built up quite a lot of experience.

The Spitfire and the Tempest, particularly with the Napier engine in the Tempest and the Griffon engine in the later Spitfires, they were the fastest aeroplanes in those days. When I first flew the Vampire, having flown these two other types before, I was rather disappointed in the performance. I expected something much more, except I suppose it was faster at the higher altitudes. They were, however, much quieter, much smoother aeroplanes to fly, of course, than the piston-engine aeroplanes, and the size of it. They were nice in that respect and more comfortable and one flew higher and got there quicker. The later ones, particularly the later Meteors, were quite a different aeroplane and you could see a much more marked difference between those and the piston-engine aeroplanes.

The jets tended to have a tricycle undercarriage, so you have a much better view and you didn't have a big engine stuck in front of when you were landing, which, of course, was an advantage. The handling was much the same on the ground, really; one probably needed to use the throttle a little and the brakes a little to manoeuvre the aircraft. Certainly, the earlier jets were a lot slower in picking up power and there was a certain lag and one had to allow for that.

The Meteors had more power and they were a bigger aeroplane and heavier aeroplane, and I think it was an advance on the Vampire, certainly. Following that we had the Hunter, which was a much nicer aeroplane in some respects, and also the American Sabre, the F-86, which was quite a different aeroplane. It had a larger cockpit, there was more room in it and it was a faster aeroplane and, of course, you could fly supersonically with it in a dive – not in level flight until the later ones where they had more power.

Before I went to the States I had flown with the RAE at Bedford with the Avro 707 and the Fairey Delta 2 and also

I had flown with English Electric at Warton in the Lightning, so I had quite a good background to what I was going to fly. The one aeroplane I did like in the Century series was the little 104, the Lockheed aeroplane. I thought was a very nice aeroplane, very fast, very pleasant to fly. I thought the Super Sabre was not such a nice aeroplane, rather heavy, but nevertheless it was supersonic. I didn't get a lot of flying in it and I suppose one would have got used to it.

I think the British aviation industry could have been more advanced. In some respects, we were but I think we didn't take advantage of some of the things we could have done. The Americans are more 'press on' in this respect. Obviously, they had more money and they had better flying facilities, better weather; all these things were an advantage to them.

I think we probably hadn't sold as many aeroplanes as the Americans were selling so they had more money to spend on their development aeroplanes, whereas we were tending to split our development of one particular specification of aeroplane. So, instead of one aircraft being built we had to spend the same amount of money over two different versions. Looking back, although this might have been advantageous to maintaining an aircraft industry, it probably was in another respect spoiling the advantages we could have had.

I had been test flying in the air force for four years. I was enjoying it so much that I thought I might try and fly for a company and I tried various companies whose aeroplanes I had flown, and I ended up at Bristol, having flown several Bristol aeroplanes in the past.

This was in 1951 and the Bristol Aeroplane Company was both an engine company and an aircraft/airframe company and so we got the opportunity of flying both aero engines on development and also airframes. At the time, there was in production the Bristol Freighter and also the Brigand and in the engine side we had various airframes that were nothing to do with Bristols but they had the Bristol engine in them and these were the Sea Fury and the civil aircraft, the Ambassador and the Avro Ashton, which was an experimental aeroplane, and the Folland Gnat. This gave me great opportunities to fly these aeroplanes. Also, the Sabre, which was in this country with the Canadian Air Force, and while I was flying those they asked if I would like to go over to Canada and fly the later ones with the Avro Orenda engine, which had more horsepower. This I was able to do and had a few weeks at Montreal flying them and had a very enjoyable time.

The Sabre was certainly an advance on the Meteor and the Vampire and it could be flown supersonically in the dive. It didn't have the power to actually do it in level flight. Then again, at this time the Hunter and the Swift were in the same situation where they could go supersonic in the dive but not in level flight. There was this difference and it just had more horsepower and the cleaner shape of aeroplane. The Sabre was a very pleasant aeroplane, I found; a much roomier cockpit and probably better equipment in some respects and not so good in others.

Had the Hunter or the Swift been out in Korea they might have proved just as good. After all, the Sea Fury did very well in Korea, although I think the competition probably wasn't all that good so I think some of the aeroplanes we had at the time apart from the Sabre would have been quite adequate.

I flew the two-seater Hunter more than the ordinary one, but not one of the very early ones.

I think the Sabre had different flying qualities. It was a very good aeroplane, there's no question about that, and so was the Hunter. They had certain little points that were different but not vastly, I mean, aeroplanes didn't vary that much. Some were just nicer and some not so nice. I suppose the earlier jets had more character.

Before I flew the BAC 188, which was the RAE research aeroplane, I got the opportunity to fly some of the other fast aeroplanes such as the FD2 and the Avro 707. I know it was a different planform, but they were fast, and I also had the chance to go up to Warton and fly the Lightning. Again, this was very beneficial, and also the Javelin that I flew had the same engines as the 188 was to have with the reheat. I flew that for several hours. They also had one at Cranfield that had the strip instrumentation we were to have in the 188, so I had experience of that beforehand.

There is a little difference in flying delta wing aeroplanes in an aerodynamic sense. The delta tended to have a much higher angle of attack on the approach. The Avro 707 was not a very fast aeroplane as one might have thought. It had a Derwent engine, but it was a very pleasant aeroplane and I found Avro aeroplanes tended to be very nice on their elevator control and they were pleasant to fly.

The RAE had got some information on the 188 but not a full story and they didn't know much about the flight testing side of it and there were certain things I had done, I had my own records of test flights but there was some of the history that I hadn't known because the original pilot was Walter Gibbs, who was going to fly the aeroplane. I came on to it two years after it started so I didn't know the early history of the aeroplane apart from the limited amount I had read about it, so it was interesting to see some of the early meetings with the RAE that I hadn't taken part in and I think we were helpful to each other and I found it very pleasant working with them.

I flew the Fairey FD2 as it was a fast, supersonic aeroplane with a different planform and handling qualities, too. It was a useful experience to fly it just before flying the 221. We'd done improvements to the systems, we had put more stabilisation in, and done quite a lot of other modifications. It had a different undercarriage because it had an even higher angle of attack on the approach and take-off, so it had a Gannet nose leg and someone else's undercarriage and it was a bit of a hodgepodge but it was designed to do a particular programme and it was very suitable for the job.

It was very nice to fly, although it was very limited in fuel and I think one of the biggest worries was trying to get through a programme with the limited fuel on the aircraft. We had a little more on the FD2 but, again, it was a heavier aircraft and so things balanced out, but it was very pleasant really. We put in different flying control units as the FD2 used to have a bit of lag in the system. We improved it but didn't eliminate it altogether.

The FD2s were flying for a long time and I think they had a version on the drawing board that could have been used as a service fighter, but I suppose it was the same old story that the money wasn't there to do it. I think a lot of our programmes were spoilt because of a lack of funds to spend on it. I mean, the

188 ended up with engines that were really designed for some other use and that let the whole programme down unfortunately.

The objectives were to carry out research in both aerodynamic and engine development at Mach numbers exceeding two and to study the effects of kinetic heating, which occurs at about 2.5 onwards. At that time the aluminium alloys were not capable of withstanding those sorts of speeds, which was why Concorde only flew at 2.2. So they had to decide what they were going to build with. Stainless steel was at that time the only material available and so it was built of stainless steel, which was difficult to handle on the shape and mould. So again, it didn't seem a practical proposition for future aircraft but the aeroplane itself flew beautifully. It was a very nice aeroplane to handle and just as well because we had a lot of trouble with the engine surging and so on but we were still able to carry out our programmes up to a point.

The surging problem was probably partly the engine itself, which hadn't been developed for that type of aeroplane, and also there was also some blame maybe due to the intakes that were on the aircraft at the time.

A lot of the test flights were done at 36,000ft or in that area. It went up to over 45,000ft and the maximum speed we actually obtained was Mach 1.88, which obviously wasn't enough, and on one occasion at that speed both engines flamed out with the surge. I reduced my height and kept my speed at a reasonable level and waited until we had done the relighting programme on the aircraft and got down to a suitable height and started them. But I think that was the start of the end.

One of the things was that the engines tended to use more fuel than was anticipated and we didn't get to the speeds we should have, so from that point of view it didn't achieve what it was meant to do. Also, we did in fact learn quite a lot from constructing the airplane, the difficulties in handling the material and we advanced the operating temperatures of oils, transparencies and so forth. These were all things that were advanced because of that aeroplane and were subsequently of advantage to Concorde.

The 221 flew exactly three years after the 188's first flight. The 221 was an aeroplane for the RAE and they wanted to try and correlate the wind tunnel results with the actual flight of the slender delta aeroplane, particularly in the transonic range, whereas they already had the little Handley Page aeroplane [HP.115], which had a very unsophisticated slender delta wing and other aeroplanes had been used. As the FD2 was available this was converted by the Bristol Aeroplane Company to this slender delta form and, as I said previously, it had other things done to make it usable in that plan. I think it proved quite conclusively the wind tunnel tests were as found in practice.

The 221 was a very pleasant aeroplane to fly. It had its characteristics one gets with the slender delta – you get the higher angle of attack for landing and take-off but once you are airborne and everything was up and going it was very pleasant to fly in straight and level flight. We went up to Mach 1.4 on it and the handling, transonically, on it was good; no marked deficiencies at all.

I think it did prove that one could fly a slender delta in various flight attitudes and speeds, in particular the transonic, satisfactorily. I don't know what other purposes it served. Obviously one always learns something from these things that one probably didn't expect. That's really where the RAE came into it. I only flew it for them to prove that it did what it was supposed to do, then they had it and did quite a lot of flying on it at Bedford.

There was a tremendous team spirit, certainly. I used to spend a lot of time in the design office for people who were on a particular project, the 188 in particular, and also with the ground crew and everyone. When both the aeroplanes came out I used to do ground running to get familiar with the cockpit and handling the engines, working with the technical people at the same time. We also had very good liaison with the RAE people, who used to have progress meetings and I used to talk with the pilots at RAE and likewise they would talk with me and we shared our views on these things.

I think a good test pilot has to be confident. You've got to have had experience with a number of aeroplanes so you can correlate between different ones and you've got to know what the objective of the aeroplane is, if it's a fighter or bomber or civil aeroplane, and you've got to know the aeroplane thoroughly. You've got to know the systems, you've got to know if you do have problems or lose a system, how you can overcome that in the same way as you do if you are an airline pilot or any other pilot but more so with a new aeroplane. You've got to know it really well and you've got to know how to interpret what is happening and be able to pass this information to the design people and talk with them and try to overcome what problems there might be.

I don't know about courage. I never had a lot of courage, but I made sure I had got good knowledge of the aeroplane and what it could do, what the systems were and so on. I always took off with confidence. I don't think it was necessarily a question of courage, particularly with the 188 with all its engine problems. I was always happy to fly the aeroplane, because it was a nice handling aeroplane, and the same really with the 221. I think if you have faith in an aeroplane, courage doesn't really come into it.

I think the British aircraft industry could have moved quicker. The Americans had the advantage of good weather, good large runways and that sort of thing, which we didn't have. Also, and I don't know why, but they had some of the German experts over there after the war and they probably went in quicker than we did. I think there was a feeling in the Ministry, or at least part of it, that we should be a bit more steady about going supersonic and all this business about the 'sound barrier' that didn't really exist.

My first time through the sound barrier was memorable in the way that we had to do it. Initially it was to fly as fast as one could in level flight at altitude and then roll over and dive down. That was a technique one had to learn and sometimes you would make a bang and sometimes you wouldn't depending on how fast you had got and so forth. But the big thing was to see a needle move to the magic figure, and certainly with later aeroplanes the aerodynamics were so much better; you could get it in level flight. Some aeroplanes would pitch up, but others were better and, again, it was just seeing a needle. No shuddering and all this business one saw in some of these films about the sound barrier.

I think we did about fifty-one flights, that is nineteen on the first aeroplane [Bristol 188], which we flew at Boscombe

Down the whole time. We did all the stalls and all that type of thing and we noticed some engine surging quite early on so we didn't fly the first aeroplane supersonically because of the clearance on the flutter, which we did later on the second aeroplane, which was slightly different but not very much so and, of course, the faster we went the more surge we had from the engine. It was a very interesting experience for me, it was a pity we couldn't do what we intended to do. It was a great disappointment to me. We had looked at other ways of getting around the problem, in fact we talked about refuelling at one stage at the top of a climb from a Scimitar or one of those sort of airplanes. Anyway, it was going to be more money to spend and I don't think it was really considered worth the while.

I think that probably it was the wrong shape for what is now conceived as probably the best-shape aeroplane. I think there were benefits in working with the materials and extending the range of the use of materials in temperature and so forth, which were helpful to designing Concorde. In fact, we learnt that it wasn't a good idea to build aeroplanes in stainless steel for one thing but this is what really decided the operating speed of Concorde, that the maximum speed they could get with aluminium aeroplanes was Mach 2.2, so it helped in that respect.

I flew in Concorde a couple of times. The first one I flew in was full of instruments as the aeroplane had not been finished. The second time I flew in it was when BOAC were doing some introduction flights and I sat in the jump seat. It was sometime after I had given up flying and I was rather surprised that I could follow all that was going on as leaning over I could see the instruments. I enjoyed that flight very much.

I didn't think there was a lot of similarity in the flying characteristics, although I suppose there were some similarities in the take-off and landing approach relative to the 221. The 188 was a very different shape of aeroplane and behaved differently. But I think at some stage in the development of the Concorde they had a certain amount of surging with the engines, matching the intakes at certain speeds with the engine. It's a pity in a way we couldn't put Olympus engines in the 188.

I think in many ways it [the British aircraft industry] was quite pioneering but I think there were many things against it. One was always the lack of suitable or adequate funds. Projects tended to overrun their budgets, and also building two of the same thing was probably wasting money up to an extent, although it was also helping the aircraft industry to maintain its hold on things while at the same time seeing which version might be better than the other.

I suppose one looks at how different it is today; the instrumentation and workload has reduced in some respects but there is a lot more to learn about how to operate an aeroplane than there used to be. It's just advancing technology and one has just got to advance one's thinking. I think so much is computerised and aeroplanes themselves are flying computers in many ways and it's a different technology. I haven't been anything to do with it for thirty years and it's quite different to me, to what I knew.

I don't think I was ever scared. I think I was more scared I suppose about running out of fuel with the aeroplanes that didn't have much fuel in them. That was the main worry to me. I think when something went wrong, I wasn't scared, I just thought, 'What's gone wrong? What can I do about it?' I then decided what I would do, and fear didn't come into it. It was just, 'How can I get home, save the aeroplane and myself and stop a disaster?'

There were two events that occurred in the 188 programme. One was after doing a supersonic run and I was decelerating and going back to Filton. The chase aircraft had caught up with me, having gone subsonic, and he said I had got my parachute out, did I know? I didn't know, I hadn't felt anything, it hadn't developed, and it was hanging out behind the aeroplane. One of our diversion airfields was Brize Norton, so I went there, although I had difficulty contacting them and so by speaking to our ops room at Filton, they rang Brize Norton up and told them someone was trying to call them up. They had gone on to one of their American frequencies because they had an aircraft coming in from the Atlantic. I landed at Brize Norton, which was fine because I knew the airfield, but one of the troubles was that if I didn't have a parachute to brake it there was a chance the brakes themselves would get terribly hot, which they did on the 188. It had fuseable plugs that let air out of the tyres to save them exploding, although this did in fact happen. I found out that I could have landed at Filton in the same distance that I landed at Brize Norton. We blocked the runway for some time and there was all sorts of talk along the lines of, 'If you don't move that kite, we'll bulldoze it off the runway as we've got a high-priority landing coming in,' and so on. Eventually, we got it off but, of course, all our ground equipment was at Filton. We did manage to get it off in time, although there was a bit of a hoo-ha about it as we had not been able to contact them in the first place but luckily I knew the layout of the place and I was able to get in all right.

I think my career highlights were when I flew the 188 and also when I graduated as a pilot as it was obviously an achievement in those days. It also gave me great joy to do test flying. I found it very interesting and flying the aeroplane was much better than flying long legs on an autopilot. I had always been interested in the engineering side of things so, to me, it was not just flying an aeroplane; it was knowing how the thing 'ticked' that I enjoyed.

I think the 188 is a highlight because I was involved in the design in the first place. By that I mean that I didn't design the shape of it or anything, but we had a very crude simulator that consisted of a television tube with little ammeters and things indicating speed and height and so on and this was all attached to the full-scale ground rig of the flying controls. I did quite a lot of flying on that, if you could call it flying – sitting on the beer crate or something – and lots of people banging about all round me. Eventually, we got a cover over it and I could concentrate better and myself and the other pilots flew it so that we got the controls we wanted and the responses what they should be and we decided to leave it at that. In fact, we never had to alter the controls at all afterwards. It was a very crude simulator by today's standards, but it proved useful, I like to think.

John 'Jo' Lancaster

Many of the pilots featured in this book began their flying careers as RAF fighter pilots. Jo Lancaster's route into test flying was slightly different in that he served as a bomber pilot. Having joined Armstrong Whitworth Aircraft as a sixteen-year-old engineering apprentice in 1935, he joined the RAF Volunteer Reserve in 1937 and began flight training. However, it seems youthful exuberance got the better of him and he was ejected off the programme for performing low-level aerobatics. Following the outbreak of the war in 1939 he re-joined the RAF and in 1941 he was posted to 20 Operational Training Unit (OTU) for training on the Wellington. He then joined No. 40 Squadron, with which he completed thirty-one operations.

In 1942 he attended the OTU instructors' course at RAF Upavon. However, on 30–31 May 1942 he, like many of the other training units, were called upon to take part in the first 1,000 bomber raid. Following a second tour with No. 12 Squadron, during which he converted on the Avro Lancaster, he flew another twenty-one operations, many of them over the heavily defended Ruhr. By the end of his tour with No. 12 Squadron, he had completed fifty-four operations. Initially, he was given a 'rest' tour at a gunnery training unit based at Binbrook but after some successful agitating he was sent to the Aeroplane and Armament Experimental Establishment at Boscombe Down. There he gained flying experience on many aircraft types in the Armament Testing Squadron. While there he was the first pilot to test drop the new 12,000lb 'Tallboy' bomb designed by Barnes Wallis:

> I completed two tours of bombers and then was able to choose more or less what I wanted to do and I was then posted to Boscombe Down, which was a major ambition of mine. I think enthusiasm was the main factor.

125

There was, of course, a general euphoria having got the war over and we had a very powerful Air Force and we designed and built some wonderful, war-winning aircraft. We had also produced a lot of enthusiastic would-be test pilots and an industry all raring to go and to make their mark in peacetime. So far as I know, most ministry contracts at that time were on a costs plus basis, so that commercial pressure was not of too much consequence to the constructors.

I think it made them much more ambitious. There were a lot of ambitious aircraft and a lot that were also fairly unimaginative as well. I suppose the Comet was one of the most famous ambitious ones. We ruled the world at that time in jet aircraft of all types.

I think they were very imaginative and go-ahead. For my own company, Armstrong Whitworth, we didn't produce many new types but behind the scenes there were all sorts of projects being designed, some of which looked jolly good to me but never saw the light of day unfortunately.

Jo's course was No. 3 at the Empire Test Pilots' School at a time when the first jets were beginning to appear:

I think we were all very excited about it and keen to have a go. The first time the Vampire arrived at Boscombe Down we were all very keen to get our hands on it. But in fact it only stayed for a relatively short period and disappeared again, presumably back to Hatfield, and it wasn't until early in 1945 before the Meteor appeared.

I first flew a Meteor in about March 1945. It had the original experimental Welland engines with about 1,200lb static thrust, which was very feeble compared with the Derwent and the Nene engine that followed. It was marvellous. It was so very smooth and really quite quiet, and I remember the first loop I tried it was at quite a high speed and I went right up to about 10,000ft in the pull-up.

On take-off the early jets were really underpowered and you had to open up fairly gently. The acceleration was probably much slower than with a high-powered piston engine aircraft but it was a much smoother aircraft and once in the air it slid along beautifully. I suppose the speed of a Vampire and the

Meteor weren't very much more than aircraft like the Hornet or the Tempest but they were much smoother and quieter. The Mk 3 had Derwent engines and so obviously the acceleration and performance were considerably increased.

There was a production line of Mk 4s at Armstrong Whitworth and they were superseded by the Mk 8, which was a superior aircraft. It had a different tail assembly and it was pressurised. With the new tailplane it was a lot easier to handle compared to previous marks.

We were making considerable progress developing the NF.11, the night fighter version. It was a combination of a Mk 7 two-seater training Meteor and a Mk 8 tailplane, and I suppose the original Mk 3 wings but the wing was considerably beefed up structurally.

The original Mk 7 had the same tail as the Mk 4 and the Mk 8 tail was much improved, it was generally stiffened. And the later NF.11 had an increased fin area as well.

It just felt like a heavy aeroplane but it had an almost equal performance. It looked larger because it had an extended nose containing all the radar equipment.

I think the ultimate night fighter version, the NF.14 with the long bubble canopy, was one of the most pleasant aircraft around thanks to the spring tab ailerons, because the original Meteor ailerons were very heavy, and it became a delightful aircraft to fly.

Certainly, the Mk 1 was very underpowered with 1,200lb static thrust but the production Derwent engines we had in almost all the Meteors had 3,500lb and with the same engines they mostly had the same sort of performance.

I didn't fly the Vampire until about 1947 when we were aware of the compressibility effects. I went to Hatfield to fly a Vampire, particularly to take it into compressibility to find out what it felt like. It was just a severe buffet that came on quite suddenly and disappeared.

Production test flying involved flying many different types of aircraft:

Obviously if there was an aircraft that needed testing, whether it be experimental or production, it would be holding things up. It wasn't done so the test pilots held themselves available seven days a week to do this work. But, of course, there were long periods in between where our services were not required. There was always discussion if you were involved with any particular project and then you talked a lot to the designers.

Jo Lancaster's career as a test pilot bought him into contact with two of the more unusual aircraft of the era. The first was the SR.A/1, which was a jet-powered flying boat designed and built by Saunders-Roe. The concept was first proposed to the Air Ministry in 1943 as an alternative to aircraft carriers, which could be vulnerable to attack from the air. But it was not until July 1947 that it made its maiden flight:

> The SR.A/1 was designed for the Pacific war to be able to use Pacific atolls as aerodromes as they were unbombable. But before the SR.A/1 even flew in 1947 the Pacific war was brought to an abrupt halt by the atom bombs and so the requirement no longer existed. It was continued purely as a scientific research programme I suppose, just the practicability of it as they'd invested a certain amount of money in the design and hardware and they tried to get as much as they could out of it. But there was no more requirement for it as jet aircraft were more manageable on hard runways than on water.

Early in his testing career, Jo had flown a number of piston-engine sea planes such as the Supermarine Walrus and Sea Otter, which were on the face of it very different types of aircraft to the jet-powered SR.A/1:

> There was a little apprehension to start with because there was no slipstream over the tailplane, which you would get from a propeller-powered aircraft, and so you were dependent on the forward speed for control from the tailplane, but in fact that amounted to very little from quite a low air speed.
> It was generally very smooth. We didn't fly it when, I think, the limit was something like an 18in sea but generally speaking it always felt very smooth indeed.
> It wasn't particularly fast. Its top speed was something in the region of 400mph but as a fighter compared with 1939–45 fighters it was fast and it was very manoeuvrable. The controls were very good indeed.

Despite its reasonable performance and handling, the SR.A/1 failed to spark interest in British and foreign services, although the outbreak of the Korean war in 1950 briefly revived interest before the project was cancelled for good as the idea had become obsolete in the face of increasingly capable jet fighters flying from their land bases or aircraft carriers.

In 1949, Jo re-joined Armstrong Whitworth. As well as flight testing Avro Lincolns and Gloster Meteors, he was also flying the A.W.52 'Flying Wing'.

The development of flying wings and tailless aircraft had challenged designers for decades even before the Second World War. But as knowledge of aerodynamics improved, the prospect of a flying wing became a realistic aspiration. Indeed, the Germans were the first to introduce a military tailless aircraft with the rocket-powered Messerschmitt Me 163 'Komet', which first flew in June 1943. The A.W.52 began life as a proposed transport aircraft powered by four jet engines. A glider version was built first before Armstrong Whitworth received the go-ahead to build two prototypes powered by two Rolls-Royce Nene turbojets in 1944:

> The first time I saw the A.W.52 was probably at Farnborough in 1948 and it was a very advanced-looking aeroplane. It was not until the following year, that's when I went back to Armstrong Whitworth, that I became more involved with it.
>
> The thing that was most difficult was the disharmony of the controls laterally. The controls were very, very heavy and fore and aft they were exceedingly light, which made it not a very pleasant aircraft to fly in that respect. In order to attain the degree of longitudinal control necessary, not only did it have to have large elevons but hard movable sections of wings called correctors that were hydraulically controlled, which was the section of wing ahead of the elevons that was adjustable to give you control over the full speed range.
>
> In order to get the controls manageable at all manually it was necessary to have very, very weak spring tabs, which meant that the connection between the pilot's control and the elevons went through a weak spring so you did not have direct control.
>
> The wing did not have a great deal of sweep back, I think it was something in the order of 26 degrees, which meant the fore and aft movement of the elevons was very short and it was some 90ft span, so that laterally was a large movement to control from one control source.

Test flying has always been an inherently dangerous activity, even though pilots and engineers do their utmost to minimise the risks. During his career Jo Lancaster had more than his fair share of narrow escapes but he was particularly fortunate that the A.W.52 was one of the first aircraft to be fitted with a Martin-Baker ejector seat:

> The worst moment in my career must have been when I ejected from the 52.
>
> This particular aircraft had, as I recall, just undergone some structural modifications to stiffen up the structure on the grounds that it would increase the limiting speed from 270mph to 350. I was entering this higher range and, on this occasion, it was a rather turbulent day, but I increased the speed and a very violent oscillation developed. It was exceedingly violent and, as I recall, very noisy. I was really no longer capable of much reasoned thought and my feelings were that the aircraft was about to break up and that I was probably going to lose consciousness, so I ejected. I did everything wrong in the ejection, but I was very fortunate because I got out in one piece.

As Jo drifted down to earth on his parachute, the A.W.52 seemed to stop fluttering and glide down in to open countryside, where it landed with relatively little damage. Jo's landing was a little harder. Although his chute had opened at about 2,000ft, he landed heavily, chipping his shoulder and slightly fracturing his spine. In view of this major problem, Armstrong Whitworth decided to discontinue its research. The second A.W.52 prototype was handed over to the Royal Aircraft Establishment at Farnborough, who continued to carry out experimental flying until it was scrapped in June 1954.

By the time Jo Lancaster retired from flying in 1984 he had amassed over 13,000 flight hours in his log book. He died on 10 August 2019 aged 100.

John Allam

There are many reasons why pilots want to move into the world of test flying. Today, as there are not so many new aircraft being built, there are fewer opportunities. After the Second World War, Britain's aircraft industry continued to design and build new aircraft as if it was still on a war footing. There were also enough pilots with many hours' experience in their log books to fill the industry's need for test pilots. Many of them such as Neville Duke, Roly Beamont and John Cunningham were household names. John Allam's route into test flying was arguably a little unusual in that it wasn't something he set out to do. But, as chance would have it, he found himself test flying one of the most iconic aircraft Britain has ever produced, the Handley Page Victor:

> It started when I was serving in Pakistan having been seconded from RAF Transport Command to a comms flight at Karachi to be captain of Air Marshal Atcherley's private crew for his personal DC-3. I was coming towards the end of my overseas tour in 1949 and I was beginning to wonder what I would do when I was posted home to UK. Looking at AMOs [Air Ministry Orders], as one had to do, I noticed that the next Empire Test Pilots' course was starting in January 1950 and I thought, 'Crickey I wouldn't mind doing that.' But reading the requirements, I saw that, among other things, you had to have a permanent commission. I was OK on that score but you had to have at least ten types of aircraft in your log book and I had something like six. I couldn't really see how I was going to get four more in a hurry and be able to apply for this thing.
>
> However, shortly after this Neville Duke arrived on the scene, having delivered a Tempest from the UK to Karachi as one of a batch, or at least the first one of a batch, that were

131

going to be delivered to the Pakistan Air Force. He had stayed for a couple of nights and I chatted to him. A little while later he came again and during the second visit, when I was getting to know him a little better, I said that I was going back to the UK soon and that I didn't know what I was going to do. He said, 'Why don't you get into the test flying business, apply for test pilots' school.' I said that I had thought of that but the problem was that I hadn't enough types in my log book. He then said, 'Well, you'll have to scull around and get some more types somehow or another.'

To some extent I solved the problem by getting Air Marshal Atcherley to let me fly one of the Tempests for a start. Then, one or two other aircraft appeared on the scene: a Dove for instance, a Viking, and so I started to build the thing up and by the time I was due to go home I had nine types in my log book.

Just before I was due to go home, Air Marshal Atcherley asked me what I wanted to do when I got back. So I said that I would like to get into the test flying business but that I was still short of one type to meet the requirements. He then told me not to worry about it as he would write a letter that test flying was just what I ought to do. His letter was going to explain that nine types was more than enough in my case, or something to that effect.

Anyhow, when I got back to the UK I had to be interviewed by the Air Ministry with a view to seeing what my next appointment would be and the interviewing officer, a squadron leader, said to me that as I had been flying all my career in the RAF, I was now heading for a desk job. No, I said, Air Marshal Atcherley has said that I am going to the test pilots' school. Oh, he said, if Air Marshal Atcherley said that then I guess you are going to test pilots' school.

It then so happened that before I went to the test pilots' school I had to renew an instrument rating and they trained me to fly a Wellington for the purpose of doing this instrument rating and so I got my tenth type.

When I arrived at the test pilots' school for an interview in early January, I had ten types and all the requirements that were written down. The interviewing board consisted of something like six officers with Group Captain Snaith in the

Chair. Group Captain Snaith had been an old friend of Air Marshal Atcherley's in the days of the High Speed Flight and he said that if you know Atcherley and he says you ought to be at test pilots' school, you'll be at test pilots' school. And really, that's how it happened.

I think that it's not terribly easy to say what made a good test pilot. You had to be able to fly reasonably well. You had to be able to write English reasonably well because they obviously expected reports from you – it's no good flying an aeroplane without being able to write a report because it's the people on the ground, the designers and so on, that want to know what you found out about it and you had to have a reasonable and sensible understanding of aerodynamics and so on. Those I think were the vital points.

Halfway through test pilots' school I was picked with one other officer to go to Patuxent River in Maryland to attend the American Navy test pilot school. This was an exchange system the American Navy test pilot school had. There were always two Navy test pilots at Farnborough and the two of us at Patuxent River. So, I was one of those.

When I came back from there at the beginning of 1951, I was posted to Boscombe Down, where I spent three years on B Squadron flying heavy aircraft mostly. During that time, although I had always considered myself a career officer in the Air Force, I became terribly interested in flight test work. Much more interested, I think, than I ever imagined I could have been, and I began to worry about the fact that when my tour ended I would probably never get back into the test flying business again.

It wasn't until the last half of my last year that I began to think about whether or not to go out and fly in the industry, where I would be able to stick with test flying for as long as I liked. This wasn't an impossible thing to do, although if you had a permanent commission the Air Force would be reluctant to release you. But provided you were going out to do something that was in their interest then they would be sympathetic. So, at Handley Page, I got to know Squadron Leader Hazelden quite well already and I was on sort of chatty terms with Sir Frederick up to a point whenever he visited Boscombe

Down and, of course, with Victor coming along. That was of very important interest to the Air Force and so when I actually applied to go and join Handley Page there wasn't any really great problem about it. It takes a little while to extract yourself from the Air Force but eventually it happened.

Although I was originally trained as a single-engine pilot, almost immediately after I got my wings I was converted to twin operations and from then on worked up into the big aeroplanes – I say big, I mean that before I went to test pilots' school the biggest thing I'd flown was a DC-3 but I was becoming really established as a big aeroplane man and then, of course, having been posted to B Squadron at Boscombe Down, which concentrated on the big aeroplane side of flight test, I just was in the right sort of category to go to a place like Handley Page rather than Hawkers for instance.

I did fly the Valiant while I was at Boscombe Down. It was a super aeroplane to fly and easy. My general experience really of aeroplanes is that the bigger they get, the easier they are to fly and so when I flew the Valiant that was, I guess, the biggest aeroplane I had ever flown up until that time and really it was a very easy and comfortable aeroplane to fly, straightaway. I just felt at ease with it immediately.

When I left the Air Force and joined Handley Page it seemed as though we were working on a wartime footing. We seemed to work every day of the week, Saturdays and Sundays, right through and I have a feeling that from the time I joined the firm at the end of August in 1954, apart from Christmas Day and Boxing Day, I didn't have a single weekend day off right through until Easter and this was the sort of pressure we were under. The thing was very important.

When I arrived at Handley Page the most unfortunate thing was that the first prototype had crashed. I was engaged to go to Handley Page before that happened, but it actually happened some six or seven weeks before I joined the firm. It had achieved a fair amount of work – not a fabulous number of hours, something under 100 hours on that aeroplane – when I joined the firm. But it had already been to over 50,000ft, it had been up to high Mach numbers, certainly 0.95 Mach number, I believe, and there had been a moderate investigation of the low-speed handling down to probably about 125 knots I think, but not to the full stall, at that time.

It crashed when it was making what we called PE runs at Cranfield – position error corrections for airspeed indicator readings. All aeroplanes have to do this because the reading you get is never precisely accurate. One of the reasons for it is the positioning of the sensor and so you had to do runs during which your actual speed can be calibrated properly, and the indicated speed compared with it and that shows you what your PE error is. It was its second flight of doing this when they were working up in the speed range and on the last run of the day – I don't know the precise speed – but the highest speed it had flown in this series of tests, the tail separated from the top of the fin and the aeroplane crashed straight into the runway at Cranfield.

It was a major upset to lose a prototype. The next prototype was very close to flying at this time and the reason that I joined the firm was because there were going to be two of them flying, they needed another pilot to assist with the programme and losing one aeroplane set us back enormously. I can't say precisely how, looking back on it now, but it really was a disaster and it just evolved as a time problem — it set the whole thing back in time.

I don't think there was any desperation about it though, there was nothing really that could be done. The second prototype was close to flying and it eventually flew in September. Its flight was delayed a little because they had to really find out first of all what had happened, why the tail had fallen off the first one and make sure it wasn't going to happen on the second one. So it would have delayed that flight a little, but it wasn't enormous.

It was not unlike the Valiant to fly in that it was, immediately, a super piece of equipment to fly and comfortable. You felt at home with it straightaway and very soon after I started flying it I was able to take it to high altitude. Quite early on I had it up to 50,000ft without any trouble, much more easily than I've ever had anything else up to that height. The only previous aeroplane I had taken to that height was a Canberra in my Boscombe Down days and it got there much more easily. The other great thing about it was that its Mach number capability was so good. It didn't have any, or least any apparent, compressibility problems at any Mach number up to about 0.93, which was really going some in those days because most aeroplanes were getting into trouble around 0.82 Mach number. Some of them, and I'm going back to Meteors, 0.78, that sort of order. It was easy to handle, it was easy to land. It had this so-called self-landing capability, which was a bit of a gimmick but provided the weather was calm and you could set it up on a stable approach and it was going to land in the right place on the runway, you could just take your hands off and sit back and it would do it and it would do a superb landing. You had a close the throttles once you had done it, of course. But it really wasn't worth anything because it could only possibly happen in ideal conditions and the conditions had to be so ideal that they would almost hardly ever happen.

One of the Victor's most distinctive features was its crescent-shaped wing:

The crescent wing was designed by Godfrey Lee and the aerodynamics team to try and achieve a wing with identical high Mach number characteristics across its whole span. To achieve good high Mach number characteristics, a wing needs to be terribly thin. A straight wing, if it can be thin enough, will probably do the job equally. But you can't make a straight wing for a big aeroplane because you've got to have structure to support the whole thing and also want space in it. In this case we wanted to put engines inside the roots of the wing and the rest of the wing was going to be filled with fuel, so you needed space inside. Therefore, the wings had to have some reasonable sort of depth. To achieve a thin wing, you would therefore have to have a long chord because the depth that matters is the percentage depth in terms of the chord. With the crescent wing what happened was that the inner part of the wing close to the fuselage was the thickest part. It housed the engines and all the structure to carry the rest of the wing. As the wing moved out away from there you could let it get thinner, so you achieved your high Mach number characteristics by sweeping it heavily. As you progress outboard where the wing gets thinner to achieve the same high Mach number characteristic you don't need to sweep it so much. In the case of the Victor there was high sweep inboard and then that cut off in two stages out towards the tip. So, the tips were not anything like as swept back as the rest of the leading edge of the wing or the inboard part of the leading edge and this achieved similar high-speed characteristics right across the wing. It didn't help the low-speed handling, but it was good for high speed and that was what was needed. Low speed had to be solved in a different way.

Its high Mach number characteristics, as a result of this, were extraordinarily good, I think probably better than anybody ever expected. There was no real indication of high Mach number drag onset until about 0.93 Mach number, which was very high in those days, and a little buffet started at about 0.93 Mach number – when I say a little buffet, I mean it was really was just a little tremor. As you increased speed above 0.95 Mach number this disappeared again and there was no further problem in that respect. Of course, the drag was building up. You couldn't stop that, it always does in these cases.

The Victor did have a wide range of speed. As everybody knows, it achieved supersonic flight, just. At the low-speed end, in the clean configuration, at 152 knots, as you reduced speed a mild buffet started, distinct but mild, and it couldn't be missed by any pilot flying the aeroplane. As we continued to reduce speed, at 140 knots the amplitude of this buffet increased quite markedly, and we used to refer to these two buffets as first-stage and second-stage buffet. As you further went down the speed range to about 125–130 knots you got yet another increase in amplitude and this was known as third-stage buffet. Eventually we had to investigate what would happen if you went right down to the stall. At somewhere around 115 knots we got a fourth stage of buffet and it was getting fairly fierce by this time. On my first attempts at fully stalling the aeroplane I arrived with the stick fully back and held back. That meant elevator fully up and buffet was quite severe, and suddenly as I arrived with the stick fully back the aeroplane pitched just slightly nose up from its position and that was that. I had it in flight, just pitched up and then immediately dropped its nose and did the same thing and with the stick held fully back it just kept going through see-saw motions. It wouldn't drop its nose to come out of the stall, which is what people like aeroplanes to do. What was going on was that with the stick held fully back the tips of the wings were stalling, or the outer portion of the wings were stalling, so, because they were behind the centre of gravity of the aeroplane, this left all the lift at the forward end and this caused the pitch up. The pitch up stalled the whole wing, so the nose dropped. But it only dropped a little bit before the flow over the centre part of the wings recovered again, gave it lift and so it went into a see-saw motion. That motion was very fierce. I recovered from the stall and made one more attempt and the whole exercise was exactly the same again. The most speed I recall seeing during any of this was 88 or 89 knots, but it's hard to say what was really happening because the airspeed indicator was flickering really over 88 to about 108 knots and the whole exercise was pretty fierce. I thought to myself really, 'This is a horrendous thing to be doing to an aeroplane and it can't do it any good and I'm not going to do any more of it on this flight. I want to have it looked at to make sure we haven't done any damage.'

I didn't know it but when we landed back at Radlett we found that the whole inner section of the starboard flaps had disappeared, it wasn't with us anymore. Now we hadn't had the flaps down during this exercise, it was a clean stalling exercise. But, as a result of all this and discussing it with Boscombe Down and the Ministry, it was decided that the Victor would never be asked to do stall trials of that sort again because we were obviously just going to damage the aeroplanes. Because of the very definite pre-stall warning that it had in terms of buffet starting at 152 knots, which was in a very safe flight regime, but not one that would interfere with anything the aeroplane ever had to do in service, it was decided that the aeroplane would be cleared for service pilots to fly down to second-stage buffet for training purposes, but in production flight tests we would clear them all down to third-stage buffet to make sure they were all exactly the same, one to another.

The purpose of leading-edge flaps was to delay the tip-stall problem to cover landing the aeroplane. Obviously, this tip-stall problem was there even with the leading edge flaps down because during those stall trials the leading edge flaps were down. They didn't prevent the stall problem at very low speeds, but they had prevented it right down to the lowest speeds the aeroplane was likely to be in flight for landing, which would be, perhaps, down to 118 knots in the very light cases but much more generally about 130 knots. So, this was the purpose of putting these things on. What they did was droop the leading edge and basically turn the thin swept wing into a sensible low-speed wing. That's what they were put there for.

They worked extraordinarily well. They couldn't be retracted by the pilot unless the hydraulic accumulators were charged up, so they could be dumped instantly if required, and they were also arranged to work automatically, so if the aeroplane flew too slowly at too high a wing loading, they would automatically dump to prevent any possibility of tip-stalling. They worked extremely well during flight test and when the aircraft first went to service. However, over a period of years they started to cause serviceability problems because the accumulators wouldn't always recharge and, of course, if the accumulator didn't recharge, then you couldn't retract the nose flaps and if you couldn't retract them the aeroplane wasn't a high-speed aeroplane in any way whatsoever. So, they became a nuisance and were causing the aeroplane to spend more time on the ground than was desirable. So, the aerodynamics department came up with a solution to this by putting a permanently drooping leading edge into the wing.

The reason they were able to do this was that we were never going to stall the aeroplane completely again. This had been ruled out and they didn't have to cover that case. But they realised that they could cover the case down to landing speeds with a drooped leading edge and that hopefully there wouldn't be any high-speed penalty from doing it. In fact, there wasn't. The drooped leading edge worked extraordinary well down to third-stage buffet just like the other leading edge did, but if you went below that problems were going to arise. At high cruising speeds the performance penalty was barely measurable and at high Mach number there was no real penalty whatsoever – from just the handling point of view. Subsequently, both Mk 1 and Mk 2 Victors were modified to have the drooped leading edge and that got rid of one of the problems of serviceability that they were having with the aircraft.

The jettisonable cockpit was a general requirement for all the V bombers from the very beginning, it wasn't just for the Victor. The whole idea was that it would be difficult especially for the rear crew members to abandon aircraft in an emergency. It was considered that the solution to this would be to have the whole nose section of the aeroplane, and that was just forward of the leading edge of the wing at the inboard area by the fuselage, to detach. In the case of the Victor, it was going to be held by four explosive bolts to the rest of the fuselage because the pressure bulkhead was forward of this. If necessary, you could fire these bolts and the whole thing fell away from the aeroplane. A parachute would open at some lower level, depending on where you had decided to do this, which would open to stabilise the whole thing and let it descend at a rate that wouldn't kill everybody inside it. It was abandoned on the Valiant and the Vulcan at quite an early stage because of the difficulties. Handley Page persisted with it for quite a long time, but a flight trial done on a glider wasn't successful and in the end it was abandoned for the Victor. However, the Victor's nose always remained bolted to the rest of it by the four bolts.

The Victor was designed to drop bombs if necessary on a potential enemy and it was intended really as a deterrent. Those capabilities were so enormous by wartime-standard bombers that they would make people think a little about whether they might attack us or not. The bomb bay was big. It was capable of carrying what in those days was the standard nuclear weapon: a 10,000lb bomb, and alternatively, in a more conventional-type war it could carry thirty-five 1,000lb bombs. It was the biggest bomb bay of any of the V-bombers and maybe the biggest bomb bay of any bomber in the world. I don't know of any other aircraft that could have carried thirty-five 1,000lb bombs in their bomb bay.

We only carried a dummy 10,000lb nuclear weapon just to make sure that it would fall out without any problems and it did; it was no problem at all. Despite the vast size of this bomb bay and the enormous opening that was left underneath it, the aeroplane behaved extraordinary well in flight both at high indicated speed and high Mach number. The buffet from the bomb bay was more marked at high indicated speed than on high Mach number, but in neither case was it a problem and trim changes from opening the bomb doors were non-existent. The aeroplane could fly in on a bombing run and open its bomb doors late if necessary without causing an upset to the bombing run and the bombs fell away cleanly. There was no problem with that at all.

I don't think the Vulcan going into service earlier caused any more pressure on the Victor, although we were going as hard as ever we could go anyway. The reasons, or one of the reasons, that the Victor was later than the Vulcan was that just at about the time the first prototype was getting ready to fly from Radlett the Ministry decreed that it shouldn't fly from there and it should fly from Boscombe Down. That meant taking the whole aeroplane apart again, and by that I mean you had to take the wings and tail and the rest of it off, transport it in chunks to Boscombe Down and rebuild it. Then, unfortunately they had a severe mishap with it during the rebuilding: they had a fire in the back end of it and this caused further delay.

But eventually it flew on Christmas Eve 1952. The Vulcan had flown back in the summer – I think perhaps June or July I can't remember exactly – but had it not been for this decision to move the Victor to Boscombe Down for its first flight, I think it would have flown before the Vulcan did. It was ready. I wasn't there for that first flight as I had gone home for my Christmas leave. We didn't know anything about it until B Squadron's hangar, which was the one I was working from, had to have a lot of space cleared in it suddenly. We didn't really know why but on the Monday morning when we came to work we discovered the reason was that it was full of chunks of Victor that people were busily starting to put back together. The whole thing was still terribly hush-hush, but then the whole of Boscombe Down was. Everything was sworn to secrecy, you weren't allowed to go outside the place and talk about it, but you could talk about it inside the place; they couldn't stop us. It was in our hangar! We began to see this thing being built. It was really quite a revolutionary affair,

I can tell you, in those days, for a big aeroplane. I mean, swept wings were about for small ones but for a big aeroplane this looked really quite fantastic. We then saw its outer wings put on with these great chunks of nose flap hanging down. That looked quite extraordinary for those days.

There had always been rivalry between Handley Page and Avro, especially at high level in the firms. It started, I suppose, with the Manchester bomber versus the Halifax and then the Lancaster versus the Halifax. There again, it was the Halifax, in this case, that was the first to appear on the scene followed quickly by the Manchester, which wasn't an extraordinarily successful aeroplane but became very successful when it was converted to the Lancaster. This was done a little bit later than the Halifax with some more up-to-date knowledge. It became a very much better aeroplane, but that's not to say that the Halifax was not a good aeroplane either.

But the rivalry was all at high level in the firms, at very high level. At one stage, and I can't recall exactly when this happened, the Handley Page design team and Avro design team decided that it would be worthwhile them comparing notes about the Vulcan and the Victor and trying to achieve the best results for the country as a whole. A meeting was actually formed at Cricklewood with Avro designers attending and discussing, or at least starting at the beginning of a meeting, to discuss the merits of each other's designs. Then Sir Roy Dobson at Avro found out what was going on because he wanted to see one of the people that turned out to be at Radlett or at Cricklewood and he said 'What's he doing at Cricklewood'? 'Discussing the Vulcan with Handley Page,' was the answer. 'Get him on the phone and bring all those people back,' was Sir Roy's response, and the meeting was stopped at about a quarter of the way through and that was the end of that. That's what went on. You would have thought people would have had more sense and that in the national interest it would be worth discussing these various aspects of design, but I know there were some people who wanted it to just go their way only.

By 1958 it was becoming obvious that the great defence asset that the V-bombers had which was altitude was not going to last very long because surface-to-air missiles were becoming available. People were beginning to think in terms of using the V-bombers as low-altitude bombers. This meant that if you dropped a nuclear weapon, you were going to be extraordinarily close to the explosion when it happened. You didn't have the advantage of height to get away from it and so it was necessary to think of a type of delivery of a bomb that would enable the bomber to escape as quickly as possible. One way was to fly in low, pull up, release and lob the bomb to the target and then make a 135-degree turn in either direction, which put your tail straight to the scene of explosion, as quickly as possible and fly away.

Other, rather more radical, thinking suggested why not lob the bomb and, rather than turn, carry on from the lob position to take the aeroplane in a half loop and roll off the top and escape that way. I think it was really a bit of a tongue-in-cheek idea but to some extent we took advantage of this thought for the 1958 SBAC Show by working up a demonstration. So we demonstrated a low-level run across the runway, pulling the aircraft up into a half loop and rolling it off the top, and the excuse for doing this was to demonstrate a LABS [low-altitude bombing system] manoeuvre. The whole manoeuvre was done entirely inside service limits for the aeroplane, we didn't exceed them at all. We used the maximum speed that the aircraft would be cleared to service for, which was 360 knots, and in the loop, or a half loop, we pulled 2G, which was also inside the service limits. Rolling the aircraft off the top, of course, didn't exceed anything, it's an entirely 1G manoeuvre, and so it just made something good to look at at Farnborough, for a big aeroplane to do. You could only do it if the cloud was reasonably clear because you went into the bottom of the manoeuvre at about 500ft and over the top at about 8,000ft and the speed over the top was down to about 185 knots, but that didn't bother us. We just rolled it straight off the top and then to clean the whole thing up for the day we made a rapid descent back down to about 500ft and flew the aircraft across or along the runway again in front of a crowd performing a 1G barrel roll and then hacked it round to land. The Victor did it and Vulcan did it, it was no problem for either aeroplane.

It was very much out of the ordinary. People didn't really expect an aeroplane with the wingspan of 110ft and that sort of size and weight to be doing manoeuvres of that sort, so it was really something quite different.

The Victor's reputation for impressive performance was enhanced further when it became the largest aircraft of its size to break the sound barrier:

For a long time, we had been working at high altitude at Mach numbers up to 0.975, which is getting moderately close to the speed of sound, and we had absolutely no trouble with the Victor at all. But eventually I was briefed to do some stability trials at Mach numbers up to 0.985 and this was considerably nearer to the speed of sound. I thought to myself, I just really wonder if this is an invitation to close one eye and let it go a bit more. Anyhow, on the day in question we covered all the trials that were required on the brief up to 0.985 and the aeroplane's behaviour was absolutely normal, no problems at all. It was a Mk 1, of course, and this was in quite early days and to achieve those sort of things we had to be in a shallow dive and mostly it was done between 45,000 and 40,000ft, starting from 45,000ft and descending towards 40,000. The dives were quite shallow, and the programme went smoothly. I just thought that this is ridiculous as this thing was obviously going to be capable of pushing past Mach 1. So, having finished the main programme, I just let it go and it accelerated very nicely and very smoothly in a shallow dive, which subsequently was calculated as being 19 degrees, and we exceeded Mach 1 indicated. Now, this didn't necessarily mean that we had been supersonic because we might have had a position error that we didn't know about. Position errors that high on the scale hadn't been measured and so we didn't really know whether or not it was supersonic and I thought well, 'There's only going to be one way ever to find this out: we have got to produce a bang and I would like to be able to put the bang down on Radlett, if I possibly can.' But this was very difficult as I didn't have a navigator on board, so we didn't have any precise means of knowing where we were or quite what 19 degrees was or where my dive was going to put the thing. But I was in the Cambridge area and as I knew how to point it towards Radlett we did another run and went to about the same indicated Mach number and that was it. There were no handling problems. Everything worked perfectly normal, the whole aeroplane was smooth, there was no shaking. There was no evidence of exceeding Mach 1 in terms of trim changes or anything at all. The whole thing was perfectly smooth, and we returned to Radlett.

When I got back I went into the control tower to see the air traffic controller and asked if he happened to hear a supersonic bang at about 11.20 that morning? He said no so I asked one or two others around but it didn't appear to have occurred to anybody, so that was that. But on Monday morning we discovered that there had been a good supersonic bang all over Watford and one or two other places and it so happened that Charles Joy, the chief designer at Handley Page, had been shopping in Watford and he witnessed it. He knew what the time was and the time coincided precisely, so there was no argument. But, of course, the aerodynamicists took all our records and this and that off the airplane and analysed them and confirmed it was supersonic and, basically, that's how it happened.

Well there was some thought about it [developing the Victor for supersonic flight]. It precipitated the thinking that maybe it would be worthwhile producing a version of the Victor that would be capable of making a supersonic dash in the target area. It was never contemplated making a long-range supersonic aeroplane out of it, it wasn't right for that and the Mk 1 couldn't have done it; it wouldn't have had the power. It had to be in a dive but with a Mk 2 coming along the possibility was not ridiculous with the power it had and perhaps having to fit afterburning just to give it the final 'oomph' in level flight to do it. It was considered but it never came to anything.

The cockpit was vastly different from the prototype to production. The prototype cockpit wasn't a very clever arrangement but that was sorted out for production.

The nose was stretched 42in on the production aeroplanes because it was carrying a moderately aft C of G [Centre of Gravity] and so by pulling the nose forward that 42in, that solved that problem.

Also, the fin was shortened by 15 or 18in, I can't remember, and that was done to stiffen it and also reduce drag because by this time we knew that the aeroplane was going to have to carry yaw damper to assist directional stability and stop Dutch rolling and the chief designer decided, 'Well OK, if we got to have a gadget like that we might as well make it work for its living and take off some of the aerodynamic directional stability hence reducing drag and stiffening of the fin making the whole tail structure a lot safer.'

The B.2 first flew on 20 February 1959 with Conway 11 engines. They delivered 17,500lb of thrust each as I recall, which was a vast increase on the amount of power we had on the Mk 1. Its engines only delivered 11,000lb each, which really says something for that aircraft because it did everything with those engines all through its life and the Vulcan always needed 13,500 to 14,000lb thrust engines to keep up with the Victor. That was just simply about airframe efficiency. But when the Mk 2 came along, that was absolutely superb with the amount of power we had.

The original Conway 11 wasn't the definitive engine for the aircraft, that was the Conway 17 and it delivered 20,500lb of thrust. That flew just about a year later and subsequently they all had the big Conways in them. That really gave the aeroplanes some 'oomph'. For instance, you could set up a Mk 2 Victor on the end of the runway and provided the radar air traffic controllers could give you a clear climb-out, you opened up the power against the brakes and at about 85 per cent power the aeroplane was going to move anyway, they wouldn't hold it. The brakes didn't slip, it was just dragging along the ground on the tyres, so you didn't let it do that. At the moment it started to want to move, you let go of the brakes, hit full power and from the moment of letting the brakes go you could consistently have that aircraft out of 20,000ft in two minutes and eight seconds and then up to 40,000ft in eight minutes. Now, for an aeroplane of this size, this was real performance without a doubt and obviously it still had plenty of power to go on up. It had a full 60,000ft capability without any problems at all. It was a super piece of equipment. It didn't change its cruise capability. Its cruise capability was dictated by the airframe,

146

not by the power, and so its cruising capability was really just the same as the Mk 1, but the engines were throttled back like mad. For instance, to cruise at 0.83 Mach number, which was the economical cruising speed for the aeroplane, you were really trickling along as far as the engines were concerned.

The Victor B.2 programme seemed to be on course and the new aircraft were expected to enter RAF service in 1962, but then disaster struck:

It is a very unfortunate story. XH668 flew very successfully through 1959 and we picked up more hours on that first aeroplane in five months than the first prototype did in eighteen months and we did a lot of work with it. During that time, we had a Boscombe Down pilot to fly with us, to be checked out on the aeroplane and so on. He was an ex-Mk 1 Victor pilot and was going to pick up the Mk 2. By the middle of August, we had done sufficient work to be able to hand it over to Boscombe Down for their initial trials. I took it to Boscombe Down and the pilot that had been flying with us had flown quite a few hours and he was getting to know the aeroplane quite well. But, he wasn't actually going to be the captain of the aeroplane for their initial trials and so I did a few flights to check the captain out at Boscombe Down and then they were ready to do their own work with the aeroplane. The two pilots that I checked out made their first flight, from which they didn't return. It was the first time I hadn't flown in that aeroplane. I had flown every single flight in it up until then and we still really don't know what happened to it except that it ended up in the Atlantic off the southern coast of Ireland and something like 80 per cent of it was subsequently recovered and put back together.

A story was cooked up to be the answer to this, but we didn't ever really know. I'm quite convinced what happened because the aeroplane was apparently supersonic down to about 8,000ft. It hit the sea with the air brakes closed and, as I understand it, with the engines at full power. I find it very hard to believe that a crew could sit in an aeroplane letting it do that without recovering, or at least making some attempt to recover. At least you would have your power off and the air brakes open to control the speed. It must have exceeded all its limits, I'm sure. But the end result of this was that everybody was extraordinarily scared of the Mk 2 Victor.

It was decided that we would have to mount some special trials to investigate the high-altitude handling of the aeroplane all over again, even though we had done a lot already and were perfectly satisfied with it. But the powers that be were quite concerned that we would lose another Victor in doing these additional trials and because of this it was decided that only two crew members should fly the aeroplane, so they would be both in ejector seats; there would be nobody to worry about it in the rear seats in the rear crew positions. To achieve this the electrical control panels of the aeroplane had to be moved to the front of the aeroplane and so they took out all the co-pilot's flight instrument panel and installed the air electronics officer's panels in that position. The rest of the aeroplane stayed much the same. It was then also decreed that the trial would consist of a set programme that was drawn up by the RAE and that the whole thing should be flown by just two pilots. So, Peter Baker and myself flew alternate flights on this throughout, each doing the same programme each time. This was just to make sure that there was no cover-up and that two pilots would achieve the same result. In the co-pilot's seat, Harry Rayner flew every single flight both with myself and with Peter Baker, so he saw the lot twice through. He was a test pilot but we trained him to run the air electronics officer's systems so between the two of us we could fly the aeroplane and run the systems.

A little while before we were due to start these trials somebody in the Ministry phoned me up one day and said that they were going to have an aeroplane watching us – a chase aeroplane – throughout these trials because if anything did happen they wanted an outside observation to see what it was that happened. What they wanted to know was what sort of aeroplane did I think would be best to chase a Mk 2 Victor? All these trials were going to be at 55,000ft and speeds up to 0.95 Mach number so I said, 'Crikey, there's only one aeroplane that can possibly do this.' He then said, 'Great, what is it?' To which I replied, 'Another Mk 2 Victor.' There was nothing else that was going to go there. He thought I was being funny and wouldn't believe me when I told him there really wasn't anything else capable. Well, the end result was that a Javelin squadron was given the task of doing this job. The Javelin's maximum altitude capability was about 48,000ft and then it was teetering and just hanging on as it were, and also it could only stay on station for about forty-five minutes, whereas we wanted to be on test condition for two hours.

During 1964, Britain's V-Force reached its zenith. Its fleet of Victors and Vulcans could fly across the globe, refuelled by Valiant tankers, and deliver Britain's own Blue Steel stand-off nuclear missile. Then, in December 1964, the V-Force was dealt a major blow when cracks were discovered in the wing spars of the Valiant. There was no option but to ground them immediately. Fortunately, trials had been carried out using both Vulcans and Victors as tankers and it was the Victor that seemed to offer the best option. Thus, the Victor fleet was adapted to take over the role as the RAF's main in-flight refuelling tankers, something they continued to perform until 1993:

> The impact of changing roles from bomber to tanker was no different for the Victor as it was for the rest of the V-Force because the bombing requirement for the aeroplanes disappeared right across the fleet. It wasn't just the Victor. We know that because the Victor was a more suitable aeroplane for conversion to a tanker it was withdrawn perhaps a little earlier so that it could be converted and the Vulcans were reserved for the bombing role. But they were probably held in the bombing role long past when they were actually needed apart from the Black Buck [Falklands War] raids, which no one could have expected or foreseen, and even then there weren't any really ready for it as they were virtually in the throes of being scrapped at that time.
>
> As a tanker the Victor performed extraordinarily well. You only have to talk to the fighter pilots that refuelled from it all the time. They just loved it because its cruising speed could be the same as theirs and it had a wide range of cruising speed, which it could easily adjust to suit any aeroplane that wanted to refuel from it. I've spoken to quite a lot of people who've refuelled from Victors and they just loved it.

During the 1960s Britain's aircraft industry went through a series of mergers and acquisitions until they had consolidated into two larger entities: Hawker Siddeley and the British Aircraft Corporation. However, Handley Page was part of neither and as a result suffered as it was unable to compete for the major orders. Its final design was the turboprop-powered Jetstream. The aircraft was a success, especially in the US markets where it provided a link from small regional airports to the larger hubs. But its success was not enough to save the company and so it went into voluntary liquidation in 1970:

> I don't think Handley Page's survival was ever certain until the day that it went out of business at least, not at our level. The firm got into difficulties in the summer of 1969 and went into receivership and was eventually salvaged, I suppose you might say, by an American banking organisation that was behind the import of Jetstreams to the USA. It ran the firm on for a while but it depended on the firm getting the Mk 2 Victor tanker contract, but since the government just would not come up with the contract and they just kept procrastinating over the whole thing the financiers couldn't hold on to the firm any longer and they just had to let it go. It was really a pathetic situation because had Handley Page got the contract to convert the Mk 2 Victors they would have done it obviously very much more quickly than it was subsequently done and at far, far lower cost to the taxpayer overall simply because the know-how was there. They had done the Mk 1s and it was the same fuselage and the same wing, for all practical purposes. It was just a case of doing it all over again on the Mk 2. Simplest possible programme, they could have had them years before they got them, in fact.
>
> There were a lot of reasons possibly, and political. I don't think they liked the fact that the firm was, to all intent and purposes, an American firm. That maybe was one reason. Another reason was maybe that they were desperate to cut down the size of the aircraft industry and it was a good way to engineer another firm off the scene. It must have been that sort of reasoning, not for technical reasons.
>
> We were flying Jetstreams up to the day before closure, up until 31 January on flight test and delivery and that sort of thing, and when we went into work on 1 February it was

announced that the firm closed at midnight. Just like that and that was the end of it. I stayed on, I was the only pilot that stayed on and the purpose of that was simply to fly the Mk 2 Victors that had been standing there awaiting tanker conversion up to Woodford and to convert Woodford test pilots on to the Victor. That really was the end of my story. That lasted through to August 1970 and then I took up with the Jetstream in an effort to try and save it because otherwise it would have gone by the board, too. There were about three of us that headed up the team that saved it and resulted in it being sold to the Air Force and that eventually led to quite a successful civil run.

All the Victors were parked in groups on one of the short runways that we didn't use all covered in whatever that covering is you put on to preserve aircraft from the weather and that obviously worked very well because every single one of them came out and with a very short service flew without any trouble. We didn't have an upset with any single one taking them to Woodford.

However, John's days flying Victors was not over yet. The demands for in-flight refuelling were such that it was decided to take some B.2s out of storage and convert them into tankers:

Well, of course, I was delighted to be able to do it and just for the sake of flying in a Victor again but also because it was the only Victor variant that I hadn't flown. I hadn't ever flown a Mk 2 tanker. I had flown the actual aeroplanes because I'd flown every single Mk 2 Victor that was built but I hadn't flown it in its tanker version and I must say I was so disappointed with it because it just was not anything like the B.2 version of the aeroplane. Immediately after take-off, my first take-off, with it I got a PIO going, that is a Pilot Induced Oscillation, which OK, the pilot does it, but the aeroplane has to let him do it and this I had never experienced ever in any Victor before that. This was due to a stability problem that had resulted from clipping the wing tips, and hence it had to be flown much more carefully than it had had to be in its bomber role. Although I didn't fly to high altitude, I only flew it to a maximum of 20,000ft on that occasion. I was told by the squadron personnel that were flying it that it was really a handful to operate above 40,000ft. Of course, it shouldn't have been. In its bomber role it was superb. But it didn't matter so much in its flight refuelling role because they didn't flight refuel higher than that anyway.

Anyhow, after my one little episode of PIO I didn't let it happen again. I had a very successful flight in it and it was very enjoyable. I spent an hour or more of the flight refuelling aircraft coming from Germany and coming from the UK. All this was done over the North Sea and then I returned to Marham. I was allowed to run three ILS approaches and overshoots and so on. I just enjoyed the whole thing and I could have just gone on doing it, super.

I suppose my overriding memory of the Victor is just to say that it was a delightful aeroplane from beginning to end. It really was. Especially in those days, one just can't realise how lucky we were to be test flying at that stage of aviation. For this country, I suppose it was the very beginning of really big aeroplanes and also the end and we were right there in it. The whole thing was a delightful experience over all the years. I don't regret one moment of it and you never felt unsafe in a Victor either.

It's conceivable, of course, that neither Victor nor Vulcan would have happened if the Valiant B.2 had been ordered and gone into service. The Air Force, without realising it at the time, would have had a low-altitude – or a better low-altitude bomber – while at the same time having an aeroplane with altitude performance that was probably so close to the Mk 2 Victor and Vulcan it's quite conceivable that they would never have been ordered. But who can tell? The aeroplane wasn't flown, it wasn't evaluated, so far as I know at high altitude that much, so it's a very difficult question to answer really. But there was no doubt, it was a very good aeroplane.

You could really throw anything at the Victor, inside or outside. It seemed to have no problem. We hung all sorts of things under the wings and a variety of things were carried in the bomb bays and, of course, there were photographic versions of it and it made a very good photo recce aeroplane because its stability was so good at high altitude. None of these things caused it any problems. Skybolt would have been a problem, if there had ever been a real desire to fit it, because the Victor was so close to the ground and there wasn't a lot of room to get Skybolt underneath it. It was always claimed that it couldn't be done, I don't think that's really true and I'm sure a solution would have come about if it was really necessary. But, apart from Skybolt, there were never really any hiccups about everything else that we wanted to carry.

There wasn't really any overseas reaction because it was government policy not to export the aeroplanes. But at one stage the South African government was interested in buying Mk 2 Victors and somehow or other it was arranged that two South African Air Force test pilots should come and evaluate it, which they did at Radlett. I'm not really sure what their decision was but when it got to government level the whole thing was stopped dead in its tracks. There was no way we were going to let these things out of our own control.

The United States eventually realised the extraordinary value of these aeroplanes because they were so much nearer to the potential targets than any of theirs and if something had really happened they could be launched, not necessarily more quickly than the American ones, but they were something like four or five hours closer to the target and so could put it in an initial strike long before the Americans could get near. The Americans appreciated this and realised the value of the V-Force immensely. I mean, the V-Force was right at the front of the whole defence system for quite a long time, right up until the rocket-delivered missiles came on the scene.

Given John's long association with the Victor, it was inevitable that he would experience other aircraft linked to the V-Force bombers:

I flew the little Avro 707 during my B Squadron days at Boscombe Down. We managed to get our hands on one of them because, although we were a big aeroplane squadron, it was part of a big aeroplane programme. I might have flown seven or eight flights on it and the whole thing was just a delight to fly. Its performance was somewhat like a Vampire and perhaps the handling was not vastly different. It was very easy to fly and although I didn't do a lot of work on it, it contributed quite a lot to the Vulcan programme and to delta-wing research in general.

Although the 707 was much smaller that the Vulcan, it did frequently give you some indications of the things you would like to know but they're not always exactly the same as a scale problem comes into it.

I had never flown a delta aeroplane before and what it did to me was to say OK, delta aeroplanes fly and you can handle them and they are safe.

In many ways the Handley Page HP.115 was no different. The 115 only had one real problem and that was lateral stability, which meant that it could Dutch roll very easily. But, having said that, the pilot could control this, he didn't have to let it happen provided you kept flying it for the length of time you flew this aeroplane; the maximum flight times were about forty to forty-five minutes. It wasn't a tiring situation to have to look after that. Having said that, and provided you realised that it was really flying on drag all this time rather than conventional lift, because it never went fast enough to get conventional lift over that wing, you had to remember on the approach to land that if you started to get a bit low on the approach, the last thing you did was to ease the nose up to try and stretch the guide. It doesn't really work in any aeroplane at all properly but if you started to get low on the approach in the 115 you just simply had to put on power to get it out of the situation and get back on to your desired glide path or approach path. But, apart from those two aspects, it was virtually a 'club' aeroplane anybody could fly. Super piece of equipment.

It was part of the Concorde investigation. Two aeroplanes, two small aeroplanes, were used to investigate Concorde problems. One of them was the Fairey Delta 2, which was converted a little bit in terms of its wing shape to look into the high-speed aspect of the Concorde's flight regime, and the HP.115 was built to look into the low-speed end of it. It really did it very successfully, producing an enormous amount of information, and an interesting thing about it was they were never terribly sure that the wing's leading edge was right and there were about two or three other wing leading edges prepared for it but they were never used. The first one was right. Godfrey Lee was good at these things; he got this one right and he got the Victor wing right.

John Farley

John Farley never lost his enthusiasm for aviation and could often be found at air shows around the country. It was at an event at Boscombe Down to commemorate the fiftieth anniversary of the first flight of the Hawker Hunter that we managed to get a few precious minutes with him to talk about another legendary Hawker aircraft, the Harrier.

John Farley's interest in test flying began when he was taken on as an engineering apprentice at the Royal Aircraft Establishment, Farnborough. However, he wanted to fly and so in 1955, rather than apply to Cranfield and learn to fly as a civilian, John joined the RAF. During his RAF career he flew Hawker Hunters on No. 4 Squadron before a tour as a flying instructor at the RAF College Cranwell. But the real 'prize' came in 1963 when he joined the Empire Test Pilots' School course. On completing this with distinction, he was appointed as a test pilot on the RAE Aerodynamics Research Flight at Bedford. During this tour he flew all the UK research aircraft then flying. As RAE project pilot on the P.1127 (Harrier) prototype in 1964, he started what was to become nineteen years of Harrier programme test flying:

> I was sent by the boffins as a young RAF flight lieutenant in 1964 to go down to Dunsfold to pick up an aeroplane, XP831, which was the first P.1127 prototype and is now hanging from the ceiling in the Science Museum in South Kensington. That was the very first jump jet that Hugh Merewether and Bill Bedford operated at Dunsfold, starting in 1960, and I got the job of taking it to RAE Bedford because the aerodynamics research flights at Bedford, the boffins there, were trying to decide whether the Harrier as it later became known, or the Hawker vectored thrust concept, was the right way to go for jump jets or whether we should go Shorts' way, which had four vertically mounted lifting engines and one horizontal engine

and that was the Short SC.1. So we had an SC.1 at Bedford, in fact we had two.

I was just waiting for somebody to tell me how to fly the aircraft. Duncan Simpson and Bill briefed me about how to fly the aeroplane and I then took it to Bedford. That's how things were done in those days – a short take-off because I had to have the fuel to get to Bedford. The engine only had a one-hour life, I'll say that again, the engine had a one-hour life! After one hour you took the engine out and you gave it back to Bristol Engines – the people who designed and built the engine – and they stripped it down and issued it again for another hour flight. Each time they took it apart there were always many blades in the hot end that had to be replaced and occasionally there were a few plates missing, so they had the servicing cycle for the engine about right.

Because they thought it was a very exciting concept to have a single extra control in the cockpit to give it all these other capabilities the SC.1 had exactly the same capabilities. But it was a five-engine aeroplane and you are flying it by yourself and you had five of everything to deal with, so while it was a much nicer aeroplane to fly through the sky and to steer – what I mean by flying is handling and it is a much nicer aeroplane to handle on the floor than the 1127 – it was a nightmare to operate because it was so complex. The P.1127 was so simple and straightforward to understand but it had very difficult handling characteristics because of the integral engine drag, which the SC.1 didn't have.

I used one of the Tripartite [Kestrel] aeroplanes to go into a hole in the wood at night, which is one of the things they wanted done, and I also used one of their aeroplanes for a very classified demonstration at that time for the Israelis because they wanted to use the Harrier as it was going to become a nuclear device for using their one nuclear weapon that they had at that time. The idea was that they would buy a bunch of these Harriers, nine or ten was the number discussed. They would each have a store on which would all be dummies except for one, and then be scattered around Israel and nobody would know which was the real one. They were determined to survive. But Hawkers weren't allowed to talk to the Israelis and so an RAF bloke who could be expected to keep his mouth shut until now was invited to fly the aeroplane for them. We did that at Bedford and we flew into a hole in the wood. They were interesting times, and this is 1964–65 – a long time ago. The government flatly refused to let them have it because of what they wanted to use it for. They even wanted the aeroplane modified so the weapons' pylons could be jettisoned after the weapons had been released so that you had more speed as you flew home.

There were myriad issues associated with getting the world's first swept-wing vertically landing jet fighter into RAF service in 1969. There were mechanical engineering issues that you can always work your way through, but there were some fundamental changes of concept required in that the P970, which is the Bible for airworthiness of military aircraft in the United Kingdom, the Bible that Boscombe operates to determine whether an aircraft is fit to enter RAF service or Royal Navy or Army service, has a little paragraph in it that says any aeroplane shall be 'stable in the circuit' and you understand what you mean by stable is that if you take your hands and feet off the control it stays where it is and if the speed increases slightly then the speed will slightly decrease again because of the stability of the aeroplane. If the height goes up it will lower its nose, that's what a stable aircraft does. But the Harrier is unstable in all three axis and has got to be flown therefore round the circuit. So, it quite clearly did not meet one of the major tenets of airworthiness for military aeroplanes. But we were able to convince people by simple force of argument and later the pilots that flew it that while this literally doesn't meet the requirements, it is ever so easy to fly and who wants to just sit in the circuit and take your hands and feet of the controls in the circuit anyway? Is that a reasonable thing to do, we ask ourselves? That might have been a reasonable thing in 1941 when the book was written but it was a brand-new concept of aeroplane that clearly didn't meet the rulebook. I mention this one specific rule but there were others, but it was an extremely leading-edge piece of kit. Forget the V/STOL, forget the jump jet thing, it was the first aeroplane in the Royal Air Force to have a head-up display.

It was the first aeroplane in the Royal Air Force to have an inertial navigation system. The first aeroplane in the Royal Air Force to have a moving map display – these things that had never happened in any aircraft at all.

John Farley's close association with the Harrier as a test pilot continued until 1983 when regulations stipulated that, aged fifty, he had to retire. During his test flying years he had been closely involved in converting the first two US Marine Corps pilots on to the Harrier. At the time, there was no Harrier two-seat trainer or a simulator.

Following his retirement from test flying, John Farley was appointed manager at Dunsfold Aerodrome in Surrey, although he continued test flying in a freelance capacity and was a regular at air shows. Indeed, it was because he defended a Russian display pilot after an alleged infringement of the rules at an air show that he was invited to fly a MiG-29, becoming the first Western pilot to fly one of these spectacular aircraft. Farley retired from test flying in 1999.

Peter Twiss

It was 10 March 1956. For the assembled team at Royal Naval Air Station Ford and Chichester as well as the crews of various RAF Meteors, the last three days had been frustrating. Streaking up and down Britain's south coast at 38,000ft, it seemed the Fairey Delta 2 supersonic research aircraft was not going to achieve its goal of flying at speeds over 1,000mph. There had been a number of technical problems, measuring equipment failing, cameras not working and 10 March was to be the last day of the attempt to break the outright world speed record.

Once again, Fairey test pilot Peter Twiss was at the controls and once again, the first run ended in failure. But on the last run of the day everything came together. Peter Twiss didn't just break the world speed record in level flight, he smashed it. His speed of 1,132mph completely demolished the previous record of 822mph set by a US Air Force pilot in an F-100 Super Sabre the year before.

Twiss' achievement was a demonstration of unrivalled British aeronautic superiority, although not everyone joined in the moment of great national triumph. Greenhouse owners across the south were agitated as the sonic boom broke glass windows. One market gardener even threatened to sue Twiss for £16,000. But none of this would take away from the fact that Peter Twiss was now a lifelong member of an exclusive club of aviators who were household names, among them Neville Duke, Roly Beamont, John Derry and more. But it is not how he imagined his career would pan out:

> I think the war brought on my interest in aviation. I was farming at the time when the '39 war started and I was obviously going to be called up so I thought I would short circuit this and put my application in to join the Fleet Air Arm, which after a while came up so I was flying Tiger Moths in 1940 – probably one of the coldest years in living memory in an open cockpit, nearly put me off for life – so I carried on from there.

159

> I had some friends who had been in the Fleet Air Arm and I met up with them down at Lee-on-Solent. They had been flying for some years with the Navy and they put over a very good case. I was interested in boats and was obviously interested in flying, and so I thought it was a good combination.

After training he was posted to No. 771 Squadron up in the Orkney Islands, where he flew a variety of naval aircraft:

> I used to do part of the flying in a Swordfish in 1941 where they had a met flight. The task there was to climb to 12,000ft every morning with these thermometers strapped on to the struts and take the temperature every 500ft and come down. Rain or shine, we had to go off in the most ghastly weather and it was the only aeroplane I would have been happy doing that in.

He was then posted to the Merchant Ship Fighter Unit on catapult ships flying Hawker Hurricanes. These missions required the pilot to ditch or bail out, in the expectation of being recovered by a passing ship.

In 1942, he joined No. 807 Squadron flying escort for the Malta convoys:

> I was operating either from Gibraltar or on a ship that was operating from Gibraltar, so it was very much in the Western Med apart from the occasional sortie down towards Malta, where we were either escorting merchant ships or escorting a carrier carrying Spitfires or some other fighters but nearly always Spitfires and Hurricanes.
>
> We also had quite a large anti-submarine programme from Gibraltar. I wasn't involved in that so much as we had some Swordfish squadrons that were doing that but for about six months we had a very regular routine of flying in a Fulmar to take photographs of the *Jean Bart*, which was a French battleship that had moved down to Casablanca after the Oran 'problems'. They were a bit nervous about this because it was a very powerful ship and they wanted to know where it was, so we were sent off about once a week to photograph it. We were always nervous about this because they had Dewoitine fighters that would appear out of the blue, but the main task was to provide an escort to the carriers and the merchant ships.

The Italians were obviously trying to do their best and they had CR.42s as their primary fighter, which was highly manoeuvrable and quite a busy little fighter, which, in the Fulmar, we had to work quite hard to keep the right side of. Later on when the Germans came down to reinforce them with the 109 then the battle became definitely Seafire material rather than Fulmar material.

I think it came down to how much experience the squadron had. We all started off with deck-landing problems; that was a major thing about the Seafire. It had a very delicate undercarriage compared to what we had been used. It was lightly built up to a point and if you landed too fast you were likely to pull the hook out of the fuselage or bend it anyway. But it was a magnificent aeroplane in the air and if you could gather enough experience then it was a first-class fighting weapon even on a carrier. But one still had to train people and it was quite an expensive process losing aircraft even if you were training them.

You just had to be able to see it [the carrier]. You had to come to a technique of landing, landing off a continuous turn so that you kept your batsman in view right down to the last cut and then straightened up and aimed to land in the first two or three wires. A lot of people couldn't get that technique and had a little bit of drift on when they landed and, of course, the undercarriage would not take drift; it had no strength in that direction at all. A huge number of aircraft written off all went over the side or into the nets.

There wasn't too much pressure, there were sharp short spells or perhaps three or four days when you were in range of the Italian or German bombers and their escorts and then you were back out of it again and outside their range. It was only very short spells. They were quite intensive, of course. They would start up at first light and go on until after dark.

I think the impression we all got was that the Italians were not forcing their hand hard enough and they put some stiffening in the whole machine by bringing some German squadrons down to show them up. But they were certainly much more 'press on', the Germans, especially the Ju 87 dive bombers. They were quite intense, those Stukas, when we were in range of them.

The Fulmar had a very good range and it could stay in the air for quite a long time. It carried a large number of rounds of ammunition; it held a thousand rounds a gun, whereas the Seafire had about 300, so you could afford to fire at the chap who was getting out of range, whereas in the Seafire you had plenty of opportunity to get close. But I'm sure the opposition realised we had a better aircraft and were much more careful about how they approached.

During his time in the Mediterranean, Peter Twiss was awarded the Distinguished Service Cross and Bar. In 1945 he was sent to RAF Cranfield to attend No. 3 Course at the Empire Test Pilots' School. That was followed by a posting to the Naval Squadron at the Aeroplane and Armaments Experimental Establishment at Boscombe Down just as Britain was entering the jet age:

My first experience of seeing a jet, I was up at Farnborough one year. I had flown in there in a Fulmar to have a meeting and everyone said to look out as a jet is going to come in and land in a minute. Here came in this amazing sight, this propeller-less aircraft coming out of the sky and landing on the runway, which was the first time I had ever heard about it – it was very secret at the time [E.28]. So that was my first impression and I didn't actually get to grips with a jet aeroplane until many years after that.

What struck me most was that it was very quiet and the fact that it didn't have any rotating propellers or anything to get going. I didn't see a take-off, which would have been even more surprising, but even landing was very impressive.

My first flight in a jet came after the war when I had an opportunity to fly a Vampire, although I did have a short flight in America in a Bell Airacomet, which was a bit of a failure because the undercarriage wouldn't retract, so I had to land almost straight away on the runway at Patuxent River. I didn't get an opportunity to fly a jet again until we were issued with the Vampire to do some flying prior to the early flying on the FD2.

As a first aircraft, I was very impressed with the Vampire. Being a jet, it was very smooth, there was no vibration. Having been flying Griffons for quite a long time, which was a robust, vibrating bit of machinery, to have this dead-smooth power there with tremendous acceleration on the take-off and sitting up in the cockpit instead of having a couple of tons of machinery in front of you so that you couldn't see much, you had a marvellous view of the runway, and flying the aircraft was dead smooth and it was a real pleasure.

I think there was a distinct lack of response, but it was more than made up for by the smooth, effortless flying, which at the time appeared good. There were several disadvantages that we saw straightaway; the fact that you're always watching the fuel gauge and you were worried about getting too far from base because you probably only had forty minutes of fuel, whereas the old Griffon would grind on for hours on end with the same amount of fuel. But one could see it was going to be a tremendous advantage; the right aircraft.

We had a Meteor at Boscombe that we used to use for deck landing trials and I landed that on the deck, but the Meteor had no problems. The other big thing I should have mentioned was in the early days the angle deck did not come in until after the war and one of the reasons for the enormous number of accidents was the inability to carry out an abort landing. If you misfired you went into these barriers, which did a lot of expensive damage, probably bloodied your nose a bit, too. But when the angle came you had this ability to abort land and fly around, which made a huge difference.

The jet's response wasn't quite so good on the power but the fact that you could see so well made a huge difference. With an angled deck you weren't quite so critical about the speed. You could afford to be a couple of miles an hour up and abort the landing if you missed all the wires.

In those first years they hadn't got all that much experience apart from the American aircraft that I had flown, although I hadn't got that much worldwide experience. I thought they were pretty well on the ball considering the problems they had, remembering in those days there were no computers, everything was done manually. If Fairey's wanted to use a computer they had to hire the facilities at Farnborough for a day and come back having done probably a fortnight's work in half a day, back to the drawing board.

There was a lot of camaraderie between the pilots and the technicians, and there had to be really because they were obviously feeling their way as far as some of the aspects of the aeroplane were concerned. In particular they concentrated on cockpit layout and the controllability and the amount of force one had to use to carry out manoeuvres and all those sort of things, and they went along with us. I think the FD2 is a typical example where we were sitting very low in a cockpit with a large nose in front of us and very little visibility and we had to dig our heels in and say we've got to be able to see more, and one of the technicians said that they couldn't put a windscreen on it otherwise the aircraft would never become supersonic. This went on for a bit and eventually the chief designer, whose name happened to be Charlie Chaplin but no relation of the comedian, was doodling a bit on the back of an envelope and said what about this? And he showed the way the nose could cock down 10 degrees so you could see very well in front of you. We were a bit sceptical at the time but we said that's fine if you can do that and we have a view like that, that will be wonderful but what about the mechanisms? He said we needn't worry about that, they would deal with that and so the drooping nose was born, which was very successful.

I think our cockpit layouts were on the whole, the worst. The worst of the lot was the Spitfire with this thing where you had to change hands to retract the undercarriage and things like that. We have never been very brilliant at cockpits. The American cockpits were generally much larger, a lot more room and space and the layouts were good on the whole.

The reason for it [FD2], I think primarily the Farnborough boys had been trying to get a supersonic aircraft into the flight test section for some time because they were being asked questions about supersonic airliners and what was the future but they had no practical experience and their thoughts at that stage were that the delta was what they were aiming at, so they obviously persuaded the Ministry to put the money forward to have these two prototypes built.

The test pilots had the opportunity of flying some of the other deltas like the Avro 707 and we didn't fly the Boulton Paul one but the two 707s we flew and we managed to get two or three flights on each of those, which was very helpful particularly from the approach point of view and the handling of the approach. We flew a number of other jets, which gave us the high-speed end of the flying, which was normally 450–500 knots and was about the most we had flown in piston engines usually in a pretty steep dive, but we were able to experience this in level flight in aircraft like the F-86, Hunters, Swifts and a number of others of that sort of the era.

The F-86 was certainly a big advance on what I had flown to that date. We were very impressed with it. It was by then in service with the US forces and it must have been a marvellous aircraft to go to war in.

In 1946 Twiss joined Fairey Aviation:

There was quite a long time between initial design and first flight because the Korean War cropped up at about that time. So the FD2 was put on the back burner because they were concentrating on getting the Gannet through and also producing Fireflies to actually operate in Korea. So it was probably eighteen months before the FD2 came back to the front line again, so it's probably about three years from the time it was talked about to our first taxi trials.

The visibility problem had been conquered and it was obviously a very powerful animal. I mean, you only had to move the throttle a small amount and you were already considering closing it down to be within the length of the runway at Boscombe, so it had a lot of power there. We were unable to do a hop as such as it was too powerful for that. We were able to get a feel of the controls, that was about all.

It wasn't a very sensitive aeroplane, it really had very good all-round controllability, unlike its predecessor the FD1, which was a very different animal. That was oversensitive and really a bit of a nightmare to fly, and we were expecting something a little bit like that when we first flew the FD2. But it turned out to be a very gentlemanly, stable aeroplane. I did quite a lot of flying on the FD1. It was a pretty hare-brained idea, I'm not sure whether Charlie Chaplin was involved with this or not but the idea was that this would be a fighter, a shipborne fighter, which would be carried strapped on to the side of a ship vertically and would take off vertically and carry out this manoeuvre and then hopefully land back on again on the ship. But it would never have achieved any of those things. It was grossly overweight and underpowered for a start. They used it in scale model form as an early form of guided missile, which they used to fire at down in Woomera and then they did some vertical launches there.

It was a little pig to fly. We were quite relieved when after about a year one of the Boscombe pilots unfortunately had a bit of a problem. He swung off the runway, collapsed the undercarriage and it was decided not to proceed with it anymore, and I think it ended up on the ranges at Shoeburyness.

We had a bit of a delay between the first ten flights [FD2] and the subsequent supersonic flight where we had an engine failure and had to land at Boscombe and did quite a bit of damage to the aircraft. It was six or eight months back in the shops but as soon as we had flown supersonically, we realised that we were flying virtually every day at beyond the existing world speed record figure. So we thought, well, if we can do this and actually do it in something in excess of 1,000mph, that will get a lot of good publicity. The directors were very keen on the idea, so over the next few months we were planning this in the back of our minds. We had to keep pretty quiet about it because we realised that the American fleet were able to, or would be able to, exceed that speed if they put their minds to it and so we had to have various cover stories as to what we were up to and why we were so secretly flying up and down the south coast.

I think it was appreciated that this aircraft was designed to fly in excess of 1,000 mph, which it did very successfully. It was originally designed so that it would fly up to a Mach number of 1.7 and we achieved slightly over that on the speed record.

One of the major problems was the fuel consumption. As soon as you turned on the afterburner the fuel consumption virtually doubled and you had to plan your flight to be very adjacent to your airfield or at least a friendly airfield at all times as you probably only had about twenty minutes if you did a supersonic flight. You only had about twenty minutes' reserve compared to the speed record flight, which was for twenty-three minutes. We were landing with about 15 gallons of fuel, which is certainly not an acceptable amount to go around, at least not enough to do an aborted landing

The record itself had to be flown over a recognised, measured course and observed – the first flight in one direction and the second in the opposite direction to take account of any wind – and the two flights had to be within half an hour, so there was no question of going back and landing and doing the next flight but there was no time limit other than that.

We did take several attempts. The problems we had were many really. One was the ground team operating the camera, which had to be geared into the timing mechanism and had to pick up this tiny little dot of an aircraft at 40,000ft travelling at about 20 miles a minute and track it through to be exactly overhead, and the people at the other end of the course had to do the same to trigger the stopping. That probably accounted for two or three of the runs being unsuccessful. From the pilot's point of view, he had to keep the aircraft within plus or minus 300ft at the height of the start and the finish and fly through an invisible circle in the sky to make the return runs. So that took another three attempts, I think.

They set a very strict routine. This was dictated by the Fédération Aéronautique Internationale (FAI), a body who sit in Paris and think up these nasty ideas.

We had to fly very accurately indeed, luckily it was a very stable aeroplane. Once it was supersonic it was extremely stable and we just aimed at this first height and then you had to climb very gradually from that very slowly because there was what they called a position error that creeps in on a petostatic system. We'd measured all this before and we had realised that as you increase your Mach number the altimeter would in fact be showing a drop due to the effect on the petostatic system, so we had to climb very gradually at about 500ft a minute to counteract this error, so that made it even more difficult.

Most of the team were very understanding about it. I mean, obviously the people at Boscombe Down, the engineers, they took the brunt of it but they weren't to blame at all. The aircraft was so small and they wanted it about six days on end refuelled and ready to fly again as soon as the aircraft landed. The technicians who were manning the camera sights had the difficult task really because it was something they hadn't done before. The timing mechanism was equipment that was used for missile work out on the Welsh coast. It was a totally different technique, so they really did a first-class job.

We kept a plotter. It was very reliable, it was amazing. I think there is a plot of the flying hours against calendar time and it does show a remarkable level of reliability. One or two breaks in it when you were going to do perhaps some routine maintenance that needed doing or some modifications fitted to it but, apart from the break after the accident, it flew steadily for the whole time.

It was extremely reliable. Quite a few modifications had to be done to the controls and the sensitivity and things like that, which it was possible to do over a couple or three days and then be flying again. We did have two aircraft, which meant we could try some of these things on one aircraft without upsetting the other one.

The power plant was a Rolls-Royce Avon with reheat, and that was incredible. The only failure we had was on the ground just prior to take-off but other than that it worked like a charm. The other failure we had in the air was nothing to do with the engine, it was fuel starvation.

On 17 November 1955 the FD2 project nearly came crashing down but for Twiss' piloting skills. At 30,000ft, fuel starvation caused an engine failure, which in turn led to a total loss of hydraulic power. Despite this seemingly catastrophic situation, Twiss managed to crash land at Boscombe Down. The FD2 was badly damaged but not beyond repair. It was this aircraft in which Twiss set a new world speed record:

Well I realised it was quite a successful one but it was in fact to be the last run. We had this amazing period of fine flying weather in March, which is totally unusual. The chief engineer decided that the aircraft had been flying for a week solidly and he wanted to have a good look at it, so he said, 'Right, this is